Y0-BQV-175

The Idea of Justice in Christian Perspective

Jan Dengerink

Professor of Reformed philosophy
Universities of Utrecht and
Groningen, The Netherlands

CARL A. RUDISILL LIBRARY
LENOIR RHYNE COLLEGE

Wedge Publishing Foundation
Toronto – 1978

Reprinted with permission from *The Westminster Theological Journal,* vol. 39, no. 1, fall 1976.

This article has been translated from the Dutch by Robert D. Knudsen and Ali M. Knudsen.

2 4 /. 6 2 2

D 4 / ʌ

/ / 4 / 0 4

may / 9 80

1978

Wedge Publishing Foundation
229 College Street
Toronto, Ontario
Canada M5T 1R4

Printed by: General Printers, Oshawa, Ontario, Canada
Design: Goodhoofd/Fretz, Toronto, Ontario

ISBN 0-88906-102-5

Contents

Introduction

NOWADAYS we are confronted, anew and in an insistent way, with demands for justice, by all kinds of political and social organizations, by ecclesiastical institutions and action groups. In all kinds of ways, in particular by way of media such as the newspapers, radio, and television, attention is focused on those who truly or in imagination are discriminated against — peoples and races, the economically underprivileged, victims of totalitarian regimes, women oppressed through the ages, homosexuals, children burdened with parental or school authority, the workman who has been abandoned to the arbitrary decisions of the industrialists, etc. All of these are groups which, rightly or wrongly, have been thought to have come by way of all kinds of historical processes into what is in essence an inhumane situation.

This call for justice, both individual and communal, is very closely linked with the entire struggle for emancipation that during the last decades has spread like a tidal wave throughout the world. At its heart is the idea of the complete self-determination and the expression of the unique identity of peoples, societal groups, and individuals, together with the idea of the complete equality and equal worth of all peoples and/or individuals.

At the same time, it is remarkable that this striving towards self-determination and self-expression, towards equality, has often been paired, as if by an inner necessity, with explicit totalitarian tendencies. That is very clearly the case with a large number of decolonialized states in Asia and Africa. These totalitarian tendencies form a common front with the struggle to establish national identity. In establishing this identity, the new governments do not restrict themselves to national politics. This identity is supposed to embrace the entire range of human existence, to extend to all of the so-called "sectors" of national life: nurture and education, culture, industrial life, etc. As a result the governments have occupied themselves very intensively with all of these "sectors," even claiming for themselves absolute authority over them, without inquiring at all whether there were intrinsic limitations to their authority. Of itself, to be sure, this is understandable; because the new governmental authorities, having been brought up within traditional tribal patterns, were not accustomed to think that their prerogatives were subject to essential limitations. Because of its undifferentiated structure, a primitive societal unit bears, to be sure, a more or less totalitarian character. Religious, political, economic, and familial power structures are intertwined therein inextricably. To this world of life and of thought the idea of a differentiated state, which in the execution of its functions is subject to inner limitations set by its own nature, is altogether foreign.

We might put the matter thus, that these new governmental authorities, even now when, to a degree under the influence of the earlier colonial rule, a typical structure of a national state has begun to take form and develop in their lands, have never completely adjusted in their political thinking to this new situation. That can make understandable, at the same time, why, altogether independent of the international political situation, their sympathies often incline towards typical state socialistic solutions to the problems before which they find themselves placed in their political and social life. Most likely they still think in terms of an undifferentiated, embracive whole.

The above totalitarian tendencies are not at all restricted to the emerging states of Africa and Asia, with their recently attained political independence. Neither are they limited to the already more established Communistic states of Eastern Europe, Asia, and elsewhere, or to lands in which Fascistic regimes are in the saddle. These tendencies are also at work, to be specific, in a number of Western democracies, where, remarkably enough, they originate and take form in an ever louder clamoring for basic freedoms and equality for the entire citizenry, with particular emphasis on individual freedom and equality. The heart of the difficulty is, that many of those who advocate freedom and equality in the world are of the opinion that the government is the appropriate organ par excellence to establish and to guarantee this freedom and equality by means of its lawmaking powers. According to them the government is called upon to push through democracy on all kinds of fronts not belonging intrinsically to the state, such as business organizations, universities, schools, etc. The state is to promote and to accelerate the independence of children from their parents; to effect a dramatic equalization of incomes; to have at heart the absolutely equal opportunity for all children and to this end to control the basic structure of the entire educational system, from kindergarten to university; to guarantee in all respects the opportunity to work, and with that in mind to obtain a great measure of say with regard to investments in industry; to establish definitely what measures are necessary in the area of health care, and to this end to be authorized, e.g., to require hospitals, even though they have a completely different spiritual structure, to enter into widespread co-operation or possibly even to consolidate. These are only a few examples. In addition, it is assumed that to all of these "areas of society" there ought to be ascribed a certain degree of "autonomy," according to the principle of "functional decentralization," and that they ought to have some input in determining general policy. Yet, at the same time, it is taken for granted that the final decision in all these matters is "naturally" vested in the central government, as the major co-ordinator of society. To it is ascribed a clear supremacy over all other basically non-political groups. In this fashion, we land up squarely, under the banner of absolute freedom and equality, with a typical totalitarian conception of the state. This clearly shows its outworkings in the socio-political activities of various Western democracies, with all of the structural and spiritual levelling that follows from it.

*

It is remarkable nevertheless that this increasing of the involvement and of the lawmaking powers of the government is accompanied by a diminishing of the task of the state in other areas. This is apparent, for example, in the area of penal law, because the attempt is made to place all kinds of acts that were previously regarded to be criminal, outside the scope of penal law, by removing the articles in question from the law books or by changing them in such a way as to allow for a much greater degree of freedom. In this connection, one's mind turns in particular to the acts that in juridical language are called "moral offenses," to articles that have to do with abortion, etc. In addition, it must be immediately added, that this tendency to restrict penal law is abetted by one of the fundamental principles above, in particular that of absolute freedom and the right of complete self-expression of the individual. It is asserted that all kinds of provisions that even a short while ago appeared or that still appear in the law originate in traditionalistic and authoritarian and as such typically bourgeois modes of thought, which are imposed by the powers that be, but which, in point of fact, are nothing more than illegitimate expressions of power, that in all kinds of ways stand in the road of complete individual self-expression and that should be cleared away, therefore, as quickly as possible.

*

On this account, it strikes us that the view we have sketched of state and society has, on the one hand, something anarchistic about it, with respect to a certain kind of human activity; but it also bears, on the other hand, a typical totalitarian tendency, insofar as the government is called, in the name of freedom and equality, going the way of radical democracy, to a task without any intrinsic limitations, with the assurance that it is thereby serving the cause of human justice. We are faced here, in principle, with "the man of lawlessness," as he is portrayed for us in the Bible, one who, individually or collectively, wishes to be a law unto himself.

In fact, the result is always a heavy handed bureaucracy, which in practice reduces the individual citizen to a nullity, one in which the technocrats and the social planners get the final say and in which there is no longer any place for a leadership that guides in a fashion commensurate with true politics and statesmanship. That is to say, there is no longer room for an idea of justice in the true sense of the word.

In this connection the study of James Burnham's *The Managerial Revolution*[1] and Joseph A. Schumpeter's *Capitalism, Socialism and Democracy*[2] is still particularly instructive.

*

The attentive reader will have observed that in the so-called social-democratic world of thought, which we have just sketched, we are confronted with ideas that we do not find so much in Marx and the neo-Marxists as in Jean Jacques Rousseau, in particular in his well known work *The Social Contract*.[3] In this work Rousseau presents the thesis, that after the loss of original, natural freedom, the body politic, as the expression of the so-called "general will" (*volonté générale*), which in this connection he expressly contrasts with the so-called "will of all" (*volonté de tous*), must bring to realization, by way of radical democracy, not therefore by way of a parliamentary democracy, the complete freedom and complete equality of its individual citizens. This work of Rousseau too causes one to see very clearly, however, that radical democracy, absolute freedom, and absolute equality are incompatible with each other. Rousseau's conception of the state has typical totalitarian traits, insofar as he holds that every law, irrespective of its content, is legally binding, provided it gives all citizens equal rights and/or imposes on them equal obligations and provided it has come into being by way of democratic processes. That is to say, Rousseau's standard of justice is purely formal, allowing no place for a truly inner delimitation of the task of the state on the basis of superarbitrary, material (contentful) criteria (principles). Furthermore, it appears that Rousseau did not hold to the idea of radical democracy in a consistent way. In order to circumvent the practically insuperable difficulties before which a consistent application of this principle would have placed him, he accepted, in conflict with this principle itself, majority rule in making so-called

---

[1] James Burnham, *The Managerial Revolution* (New York: The John Day Co., 1941).

[2] Joseph A. Schumpeter, *Capitalism, Socialism and Democracy* (New York and London: Harper and Bros., 1942). German trans., *Kapitalismus, Sozialismus und Demokratie* (Bern: A. Franke, 1946).

[3] Jean Jacques Rousseau, *Du contrat social ou principes du droit politique*. Eng. tr.: *The Social Contract* (Chicago: H. Regnery, 1954).

democratic decisions. The idea of majority rule, however, is completely at odds with his central thoughts. I shall return to this and other points later on.

Democratic socialism, which has been inspired by Rousseau among others, is, in the final analysis, no real servant of justice, even though it, no doubt in good faith, has sought to be. Abolishing in principle the unique, original responsibility of all kinds of other societal structures, it hands society over to the all devouring state leviathan.

Does the foregoing have as its consequence that we are pushed in the direction of a liberal individualism in the spirit of John Locke, who saw as the highest and proper task of the state the protection of the individual freedoms and rights of its citizens and the "laissez-faire laissez-passer" politics of the classical school of economics, of men such as David Ricardo and Adam Smith? History, in particular that of various Western European lands in the nineteenth century, has clearly shown us that this way too does not lead us to a truly just and free society. The freedom that was proclaimed seemed to accrue only to the benefit of the few, while, as a consequence of the so-called free play of economic forces, a very large proportion of the populace landed up in a true slavery of labor. Under the influence of the Enlightenment thought of the 18th century, the individualistic liberals of the 19th century had an overly optimistic view of man. They completely underestimated the sinful inclinations of man. Therewith they also misconstrued the very essential, multiform task that government has to fulfill by reason of its divine calling in this real world, broken as it is by sin, in the interests of the weak members of society, individuals as well as groups and communities.

*

In what precedes there is, as I see it, reason enough to reflect more closely on this problem area, indeed, in particular, on the idea of justice. In doing this I shall hold myself to the following major topics: 1) the idea of justice in ancient times; 2) the idea of justice in Western humanistic thought; 3) the idea of justice in Christian thought; 4) a critical recapitulation; 5) justice and the principles contained in it as dynamic forces in the continuing process of making laws in a pluralistic society.

1. Ancient Thought

The idea of justice has a long history in Western thought, from ancient Greece to modern times, inside as well as outside of Christian circles. For the most part it is connected with the idea of a cosmic or natural order. It is designated by various terms: *ordo naturalis* (natural order), *lex naturalis* (natural law), *lex aeterna* (eternal law), *ordo divina* (divine order), *lex divina* (divine law), etc.

Already in pre-Socratic Greek philosophy there appear so-called natural law conceptions in Anaximander, Heraclitus, Parmenides, and the Pythagoreans. They originate in the idea that there is an established, unchangeable order that cannot be escaped, in which there is manifest a retributive justice, and which impresses itself as such on man.[4] By reason of this order there pertains in nature an equilibrium between coming into being and passing away. Things that take on an individual bodily form do injustice to each other, because they can maintain this form only at the expense of other temporal things. But they make amends for this injustice by their dissolution. So taught Anaximander and Heraclitus. Both are oriented in their thought to the primitive legal commerce between the blood related communities of their time. Here we are confronted with the so-called nature- or matter-motive, which originally played the key role in Greek religion, and with it in Greek culture and Greek thought.[5]

The situation changes drastically with Parmenides, the founder of the Eleatic school. He too connects the ideas of right and necessity, both of which undergird an order of justice in all of nature. He does not, however, ascribe the primacy to the nature- or matter-principle, but to the so-called form-principle, which in

---

[4] In composing the following survey of the idea of justice in ancient and in modern humanistic thought, I have gratefully made use, among other sources, of Herman Dooyeweerd, *Encyclopaedie der rechtswetenschap*, I: *Inleiding en Historisch gedeelte*, and H. J. van Eikema Hommes, *Hoofdlijnen van de geschiedenis der rechtsfilosofie* (Deventer: Kluwer, 1972). In writing his book Hommes has used and has enlarged upon the first volume of the aforementioned work of Dooyeweerd, just as in his book *De elementaire grondbegrippen der rechtswetenschap: Een juridische methodologie* (Deventer: Kluwer, 1972) he has made extensive use of the second volume of the same syllabus (the thetical part).

[5] Hommes, *Hoofdlijnen van de geschiedenis der rechtsfilosofie*, p. 5.

later times begins to play a key role in Greek life, in a broad sense. This is the case, be it that he naturalistically still connects this principle of form with the invisible form of the firmament. Justice (*dikē*) and necessity or fate (*anangkē*) hold "being" firmly in the grip of its perfectly spherical form and protect being from not originating or from passing away. That is to say, if being should transgress its limit (i.e., form), it would land up in the domain of "non-being." Within this pattern of thought, therefore, "being" and "becoming" (as a kind of "non-being"), the form-principle and the matter- or nature-principle, come to stand in a dialectical, essentially insoluble tension with each other. Common to these conceptions, however, is the thought that law is not restricted to human society but embraces reality in its entirety. Human laws too are regarded to be a part of the divine or natural order, insofar as it, as Heraclitus taught, is nourished by the one divine law. So-called positive law, as an expression of the divine law, is completely binding for the populace. Here there is still no place for any tensions or opposition between natural and positive law, with which we are continually confronted in later theories of natural law.[6]

*

The latter changes with the emergence of the Sophists in the fifth century. Their rise is most intimately connected with the consolidation and the blossoming of the Greek city states. In these city states (*poleis*) we no longer have to do with the ancient tribal organization (*phylai*), brotherhoods (*phratrai*), and clans (*genē*), but with a territorial political organization, within which the so-called differentiated city law had superseded the older undifferentiated law of the consanguineal groups. Concurrently a heavy accent came to rest on human lawmaking. More broadly expressed, in the life of the Greek city state the religious principle of matter or nature in Greek religion had to give way before the so-called principle of form.

The preceding had as a result, among other things, that it became of critical importance to influence public opinion. This brought the Sophists and in particular the founder of the movement Protagoras even to the point of asserting that man is the measure of all things (*pantoon chrēmatoon metron anthropos*). As a consequence, the idea prevalent up to that time of an eternal

[6] *Ibid.,* pp. 6–7.

natural order, which also controls human society, was in principle undermined. It is first in the city state that human nature receives cultural forming by means of education and obedience to positive law. All law is *positive* law and depends for its establishment on the appropriate institutions of the state. No longer is there a super-arbitrary order that underlies reality and that is likewise in principle constitutive and regulative of positive law. One can view the Sophists as such as the predecessors of the later legal positivists. In Protagoras and his followers the content of positive law is in point of fact dependent upon the position of strength of those who are able to impress upon the people their opinion concerning what is good and bad, what is just and unjust, and know how to influence decisively in a continuing way the formation of law.[7]

*

It was in particular Socrates who set himself against the influence of the Sophists, which was undermining all the foundations of Athenian society. He saw the true end of man as a virtuous life in the city state, in obedience to its written and unwritten rules. In this obedience one also depends on intuitive knowledge (*theooria*) of the idea of the beautiful and the good. And because an upright life depends upon knowledge, no one acts wrongly if he comes to the true knowledge of the good and the beautiful, by virtue of the divine spiritual power resident within him, the imperishable self, in which the divine "nous" manifests itself in man. This explains why for Socrates acting virtuously is, in the final analysis, dependent upon self-knowledge.

For Socrates, therefore, the standard of human action did not reside in man himself but in the regulative idea of the beautiful and the good. In this the religious principle of form of Greek religion, in its central meaning, was valid, according to him, also for human action. Thus he returned to the "forms of being" behind the world of sense experience.

*

The ideas that were developed by Socrates, primarily with an eye to the practical life of the Greek cities, were worked out, particularly by Plato and Aristotle, in a more metaphysical, speculative spirit.

[7] *Ibid.*, pp. 7ff.

As it is well understood, Plato made a sharp distinction between the world of changeable things that are perceptible to the senses (*phainomena*) and the world of the super-temporal, supersensory ideas (*eidē*), which can be known only by way of theoretic contemplation (*theooria*), with the understanding that the ideas or ideal forms of being function as models for the temporal things subject to change, temporal things being only shadows of the ideas.

In a later period, Plato views these ideas as simple, unchangeable, and eternal forms of being. These he relates concentrically, in the line of Socrates, to the idea of the beautiful and the good, which he identified with divine reason (*nous*), which generates the forms of being and makes them knowable by rational thought.

To the world of the ideal forms of being belongs also the idea of justice. As was the case with earlier thinkers also, the validity of this justice is not restricted to human society; it extends also to the human soul and to the cosmos in the wider sense (*makrokosmos*).

Analogous to the composition of the human soul, the ideal and just city is now composed out of three orders: The highest is that of the philosophers. They rule the state, equipped for their task by their knowledge of the absolute ideas. The second order is that of the military, with their characteristic virtue of bravery. These two orders function exclusively in the domain of civil justice. They must dedicate themselves to serving the public interest of the city state. Finally, the third order is that of the farmers and artisans. This order, in contrast to the other two, knows private family and property relations and has the care of providing for the economic needs of the society. In every respect this order is subordinated to the first two. It does not have a typical civil-legal status.

Justice is comprised in this, that every order performs the task proper to it and makes its contribution to the life of the entire state.

Plato's conception of the state possesses an explicit totalitarian character. For freedom and equality, as we described it in our introduction, there is no place.[8]

---

[8] For a study of the development of Plato's thought, see H. Dooyeweerd, *Reformatie en Scholastiek in de wijsbegeerte*, I: *Het Grieksche voorspel* (Franeker: T. Wever, 1949), pp. 175ff. Cf. Hommes, *op. cit.*, pp. 12ff.

In Plato's later development, there comes to expression a clear tension between the idea of justice, as it is enunciated in the state by the philosophers, and so-called positive law, namely, law as it actually pertains. This tension is a result of a more universal one, between the absolute forms of being, the ideas, and the perishable world of matter. This in turn depends on the dialectical ground motive of Greek religion, with its intrinsically irreconcilable polarity of the world of forms (ideas) and the world of matter.[9]

Originally Plato was opposed to a general law code in the state. The philosophers, who as such were entrusted with leading the state, were supposed to rule it on the basis of a concrete viewing of the world of ideas. Later, however, Plato advocates the need for a general law code in the state, one that was supposed to establish a balance between freedom and order. It is a question of finding the proper mean between the ideal just state and a state which has succumbed to an arbitrary tyranny or anarchy. In this connection, the question is not in the first place one of establishing external guarantees of the spheres of freedom of the individuals. Rather, lawmaking must seek to lead the citizens to a virtuous and complete life. Therefore Plato lays strong emphasis on the meaning of the preambles to the laws. Therein the true foundations and goals of the law must be stipulated. In this the body politic remains at the center. There is no possibility then of acknowledging the unique competency and responsibility of bonds independent of the state. The individual is absorbed, with his entire existence, in the state community. Neither individuals nor social groups as such can establish laws and privileges *in opposition to* the state community. Even the so-called legal commerce between the citizens, insofar as it is permitted, is ultimately determined by the civil authorities.

*

We also discover the same totalitarian leanings in Aristotle, be it that his conception differs sharply from that of Plato.[10] According to Aristotle, the ideas do not belong to a separate *transcendent* reality. Instead, they are *immanent* essential forms, which give a concrete form to matter, which is from the begin-

---

9 Hommes, *op. cit.,* p. 14.
10 *Ibid.,* pp. 16ff.

ning formless. Matter, in itself formless, first obtains actual existence *in connection with* the immanent ideas or essential forms, which are themselves the product of divine reason (*nous*) and as such give direction to individual things (as a substantial union of originally unformed matter and substantial essential form). In reality, therefore, we have to do with a continual progression from potential to actual being, a process that has its deepest ground in the divine reason as the first, itself unmoved mover of the universe.

According to Aristotle, therefore, everything strives, according to its own essential form, towards its own realization. But, at the same time, conformable to the teleological order that is present in (rationally determined) reality, everything in its composition of originally unformed matter and substantial essential form functions in turn as matter, as a building material, for something higher, in a relation of means to end, with the understanding that this so-called teleological order has its ultimate goal, its ultimate destination, in this divine reason (*nous*).

We also encounter such a "teleological order," according to Aristotle, in human society. There too he discerns a hierarchical framework, from the lowest social unit, the so-called family unit, by way of the community, which is determined especially by economic goals, to the city state (*polis*). The lower communities, therefore, have their highest destination in the state, which according to its inner telos is the highest community and is as such completely self-sufficient. For Aristotle then man is a completely social being, a *zoon politikon*. That involves, at the same time, that the supreme moral virtue consists in obedience to the written and unwritten laws of the city state. It also involves that justice and the order of law coincide with order as it is brought into being by the state.

With regard to the law of the state Aristotle makes a clear distinction between *natural law* and *positive law*. By natural law he understands those laws for society that hold altogether independent of any positivizing activity of man. They have as such equal validity everywhere, independent of whether they are accepted by man. So-called positive law lacks this absoluteness as to what concerns its content; but once established it ought to be obeyed. Establishment by man is determinative, therefore, for positive law. Here, however, the civil authorities have a decisive voice.

*

It is first with the Stoics that there emerges the idea of a world community. It departs from the more or less classical Greek distinction between the Greeks, on the one hand, as citizens with full rights, and the barbarians, on the other hand, as in essence people without any rights whatsoever.[11]

The development of this thought, just as, for that matter, the development of the fundamental thoughts of Plato and Aristotle, did not occur in isolation from the historical situation of the time, i.e., the rise of the empire of Alexander the Great, as a result of which the traditional political boundaries of the Greek world were extended in every direction.

Central to the thought of the Stoics is the idea of the *immanent world logos,* in the sense of an immanent cosmic order or natural law. Cosmic reality as a whole has its ground in the forming activity of divine reason (*logos, nous*) by way of emanation. This world logos reveals itself in all things and brings these together into a dynamic unity. Thus also man participates in divine reason.

The preceding involves that man no longer has to prove his ultimate loyalty to the order, the system of law, of the state, but to the natural law of the divine logos, which is immanently at work in reality and which also comes to expression in human reason. Man also has the obligation, therefore, to be true to himself and therein to express and preserve himself. Although the Stoics do not do away with community life, they assert that man can come to complete expression independently of it. If all men participate equally in the divine logos, that is to say, can come to complete expression in it, all of them without exception are in principle equal and form a single great universal community, which includes the entire world, one that is maintained in existence by divine reason or natural moral law.

Here we come across ideas that will later be incorporated into Western humanism. They preserve, however, their own colora-

[11] *Ibid.,* pp. 27ff.

tion, which in important respects is determined by the spiritual climate of the time. The community appears to work *in a forming way* on a segment of unordered life (matter?).

In this connection it is important to point out that Seneca, for example, drawing on Stoic thought patterns, makes a distinction between an original, natural state of innocency (cf., Jean Jacques Rousseau, e.g., within Western humanistic thought), in which all men are equal and in which there is an absence of coercion, and the situation, brought into being by human evil, of civil coercion, slavery, and private property, institutions that must provide needful services, so that one may live a virtuous life in the present world. From this it appears that Seneca viewed the state as described by the Stoics, which has complete freedom and equality of its citizens, as more of an ideal than a reality. In sharp contrast to this idea of the ideal state, there is still his more or less totalitarian and absolutistic conception of the authority of the ruler. For, although Seneca holds that the state is overarched by a world-wide community of gods and men, the ruler exercises authority in the state as a god who can dispose over his subjects body and soul. The ruler is the source of all positive law and is at the same time the soul of the state as an all-inclusive temporal community.

Apparently, in order to avoid fragmentization in human society, Seneca searches nevertheless for an ultimate concentration point for this human community, because of the law of concentration operative in this world and as a consequence also in our thought. Failing to discover a concentration point outside, he discovered it within this reality, namely, in the state, for which apparently the Stoic idea of world citizenship has to make way.

2. Renaissance and Western Humanism

The idea of a natural law that is valid independently of time and place and thereby of human positivization has also gotten a substantial place in Western humanistic thought. Likely this may be viewed as a reaction to the doctrine of *Staatsraison,* which was defended, e.g., by Machiavelli, just as during the period after the Second World War, particularly in Germany, there was a renaissance of the idea of natural law.[12] In this connection we can mention the names, e.g., of Hugo Grotius, Samuel Pufendorf, Christian Thomasius, John Locke, Christian Wolff, as well as Jean Jacques Rousseau and Immanuel Kant.

*

As it is known, Hugo Grotius was the founder of international law. He developed his ideas in particular in his well known work, *On the Law of War and Peace* (*De jure belli ac pacis*). Central to this work was the question of the just war. Earlier, in his *The Freedom of the Seas* (*Mare liberum sive de iure quod Batavis competit ad indicana commercia*), he had given his attention to another important and very pertinent question of international law.

Grotius begins with the thought that in international law we have to do with two kinds of things, namely, natural law and positive law, the second of which is established explicitly or implicitly by means of a contract. According to him, natural law holds both for the individual and for the nations in their commerce with each other.

Grotius developed his thought about natural law in the spirit of the newly developed way of mathematical thinking, the mathematical ideal of science of Western humanistic thought. He attempts to develop his system of law without taking into consideration directly the particular legal relationships as they actually pertain. His method, therefore, is purely deductive, after the fashion of geometry (*more geometrico*). In this he begins with the principle that man, in distinction from animals and plants, possesses an urge to live peaceably with his fellow man (*impetus socialis*). In this we have to do with an objective natural foundation, which is not subject to human vagaries. Striving to attain to a peaceful community is, at it were, natural to man, incorporated in him.

Proceeding in terms of the above fundamental principle, Grotius develops four additional principles:

a. the principle of mine and thine, which teaches us that we must refrain from taking what belongs to someone else and that

[12] See H. J. Hommes, *Een nieuwe herleving van het natuurrecht* (Zwolle: W. E. J. Tjeenk Willink, 1961).

we, insofar as we come into possession of such goods, must pay for them;

b. the principle that we must honor agreements (*pacta sunt servanda*);

c. the principle that we must compensate for damages that we have caused by our own fault;

d. the principle that violations of natural and positive law must be punished.

What is striking about Grotius' conception of natural law is its typical individualistic trait. It takes as its starting point the particular individuals who come into contact with each other in the so-called state of nature and the consequences that are bound up with this so-called "social" intercourse. In Grotius' natural law theory we have to do with a kind of commutative justice, in distinction from distributive justice, which presupposes a community. We shall give further attention later on to this idea, which has such a prominent place in the thought of Thomas Aquinas. Grotius' natural law theory, in fact, focuses on the idea of civil right. This idea, namely, presupposes that individuals and groups within the state juridically speaking stand on an equal footing with each other. That is to say, they do not stand in typical hierarchical relationships. In the further outworking of his juridical thought, Grotius tied in closely with Roman law, which at that time had been received into various European lands. This he viewed as codified reason (*ratio scripta*).[13]

It is important to note that Grotius' natural law theory has a realistic character. He goes out from the thought that the natural law developed by him would be valid even if it should be allowed — which, for that matter, he considers to be a blasphemy — that no God exists or that he does not concern himself with human affairs. Put otherwise, Grotius' conception of natural law bears a typical rationalistic cachet. In it there comes to expression the apparently irresistible influence of the humanistic ideal of science. Natural law, in the last analysis, is a product of human reason. That does not take away from the fact, as Hommes has correctly observed, that Grotius acknowledges to some degree the Christian idea of creation, when he says that natural law, even

---

[13] Hommes, *Hoofdlijnen*, pp. 69ff.

though it derives from principles innate to man, must nevertheless be ascribed to God, because he willed that such principles should exist within us. Hommes points out, with reference to a statement in *De iure belli ac pacis* (Lib. I, cap. I, 10, 1), that according to Grotius it is the case that God himself is bound to natural law.[14]

Now the state too, Grotius maintains, is founded in natural law, indeed in particular in the principle that contracts must be honored. All the rights of the state, namely, are derived from an original contract, by means of which the state is formed. Grotius sees the relationship between natural law and the positive law of the state in this way, that positive law can never require what natural law forbids or forbid what natural law requires. Natural law, therefore, forms the exclusive framework within which positive law can move. It functions also in particular where so-called positive law cannot provide a solution.

But, and in this connection there comes into play a very strange element in the thought of Grotius, natural law, which functions as an intrinsic limit to positive civil law (*ius civile*) may be *nullified* if that is required by the *general welfare of the state*. In the meanwhile, the establishment of what is in the general interest of the state is the exclusive prerogative of the ruler. Further, the ruler is even authorized to set aside the established rights of his subjects because of the superior dominion ascribed to him.

In Grotius' thought we are confronted, therefore, with a major and in essence irreconcilable tension between the general welfare of the state and natural law. Here there is no longer any question of an essential, inherent limitation of the task of the state, which flows out of its super-arbitrary nature and structure. Even the natural law advocated by Grotius must give way before the *Staatsraison*. In this sense Grotius' thought displays a common levelling tendency. It is not able to give an account of the great variety of structures in human life.[15]

*

John Locke supposed that he had discovered this limitation. He sought it, namely, in limiting the goals of the state.

[14] *Ibid.*, pp. 78–79.
[15] *Ibid.*, pp. 80ff.

John Locke takes his starting point in the inalienable natural rights and freedoms of man. In the first volume of his *Two Treatises of Civil Government,* Locke opposes the absolutistic theories of the state set forth by Robert Filmer. Locke proceeds in terms of a supposed state of nature, in which individuals live under the authority of unchangeable laws of nature. He takes a nominalistic standpoint. For him, therefore, the relationships between individual things are not realities apart from man but are only the product of human thought. That holds also for the relationships between men.

For Locke so-called natural law is a body of normative relationships between men considered as standing on their own, in a state of nature, which itself is a product of human thought. By reason of the law of nature violations of individual rights may be punished by anyone, while the right of compensating for damages is the prerogative only of the proper authorities. This means, according to Locke, that the law of nature and the natural rights of the individual have truly the character of law. Natural law as such is superior to the positive law of the state. It determines also as such the relationships between the states that still find themselves in a state of nature.

In agreeing to a so-called social contract, individual men emerge from the state of nature. They do that because, on the basis of the insight provided by their natural reason, they do not consider the state of nature to offer sufficient guarantees, even though Locke describes it as a state of peace. Calling into existence a so-called civil state occurs, therefore, in order to surround the original freedoms and rights with additional guarantees. In making this contract individuals do not transfer all of their rights to the state, which was the position set forth, as we shall later see, by Rousseau. They hand over only their natural right of inflicting punishment. In place of taking the law into his own hands, one receives the protection of the civil magistrate and the courts of the freedom and rights which accrue to him in the state of nature and which retain their natural character, even after the institution of the state. There is here a clear delimitation, therefore, of the task of the state, namely, protecting the inalienable natural human rights and freedoms of the individual.

Locke's theory of the state suffers, however, from an obvious weakness. Possibly it is better to put the matter in this way, that both his view of the state and of society, indeed his entire vision of human society, suffers from a fundamental weakness, in that he has room only for two poles, namely, individual persons and society, more specifically, the state. In his account of the structure of society, Locke does not in any way give account of the unique character and structure and thereby of the unique responsibilities of the various typical associations other than the state. Considered in this way, Locke's view of the state and of society, just like that of Grotius, *levels* structural differences and is fundamentally atomistic and individualistic in character. Thus Locke is indeed the founder of the liberal, individualistic conception of the state, as this has become politically dominant, particularly in the nineteenth and part of the twentieth centuries, in a number of Western lands, to the detriment of millions. This view still controls in part political life in the United States. This liberal individualistic view of the state misconstrues, as we have earlier observed, the profound influence of sin on society. In addition, it does not have an eye for the unique and extensive task of state government by reason of its peculiar calling in society. In particular, the state is called upon to establish public justice, which involves far more than protecting individual freedoms and rights. The idea that just relationships will emerge in society as of themselves through the so-called free play of forces is nothing more than a fiction.[16]

*

In opposition to this liberal, individualistic conception of John Locke, Jean Jacques Rousseau, even though he too started with an original state of nature in which individuals mutually enjoyed in complete harmony the natural freedoms and rights that were properly theirs, went nevertheless in a radically different direction, namely, that of a collectivism.[17]

[16] *Ibid.,* pp. 111ff. For a profound analysis of Locke's philosophical views concerning the state and law see J. P. A. Mekkes, *Proeve eener critische beschouwing van de ontwikkeling der humanistische rechtsstaatstheorieën* (Utrecht and Rotterdam: Libertas, 1940), pp. 200–229.

[17] See Jean Jacques Rousseau, *The Social Contract.* Original French, *Du contrat social ou principes du droit politique,* first published in 1762. For a profound analysis of Rousseau's thought see the book of Mekkes cited in note 16, *Proeve eener critische beschouwing,* pp. 266–314.

As we have already remarked, the ideas of Rousseau are still very relevant, because in them there was an attempt to bring into a unity the ideas of freedom, equality, radical democracy, and collectivity.

Rousseau, in developing his conception, took as his starting point the idea of the original goodness of man. Society, however, has been corrupted by science and culture. There is, however, no way to rectify this situation. A new society must be established, therefore, on the foundation of a social contract. According to the terms of this, for that matter, fictional contract, men must hand over everything they have, that is to say, their original, natural rights and freedoms in their entirety, to the new society, to the end that within this community they might receive them back again in a higher form, namely, as civil ones. To this end they are supposed of their own free will to place their entire person and everything pertaining thereto under the direction of the general will, the *volonté générale*.[18] In this fashion there comes into being a moral and collective body, which is not simply a collection of individuals but which possesses its own collective I and its own life and will, which are clearly distinct from the life and will of the individual citizens, from the *volonté de tous*.[19]

In this newly founded community complete sovereignty is ascribed to the people organized therein as a whole. It is as such inalienable and cannot be delegated to the government, not even to a parliament. In this sovereignty the general will of the people expresses itself. This general will is so universal, that it cannot tolerate the existence of any single particular will beside it. This implies that every law has to give equal rights to the citizens and must impose equal burdens upon them. As soon as this pertains, every law, irrespective of its material content, is legally valid.

In Rousseau's thought the following are central: the idea of freedom, which men receive back again within the state in a higher form; human self-determination, which in the form of radical democracy is retained even within a totalitarian state; and the equality of all citizens without exception before the law.

At that the question remains, how the laws came into existence.

18 Rousseau, *op. cit.*, Book I, chapter VI.
19 *Ibid.*, Book I, chapter VI.

As we saw, Rousseau does not want to acknowledge an independent lawmaking power. Such a power comes into conflict with the idea of the complete sovereignty of the people. Rousseau discovers the following solution.

He starts out with the assumption, that the sovereign people, as the embodiment of the general will, can never hurt a single one of its individual members, even though that will not always be experienced as such by every single citizen. In such a case the individual citizen will have to accommodate himself to the general will of the sovereign people, that is to say, according to the general will as this has been established by majority rule. And that ought to happen under the motto — and therein resides, as it were, the entire dialectic of Rousseau's thinking, one that is incapable of any immanent solution: "On le forcera d'être libre," "One shall force him to be free."[20] Rousseau can save himself from the impasse into which he threatens to come as a result of his radical democratic starting point only by introducing something foreign to his thought, i.e., the mathematically oriented idea of a democratic majority, in which there again appears the counterpole of the humanistic personality ideal represented by Rousseau's thought.

The result of the one and the other is that Rousseau emerges with a totalitarian idea of the state, that is to say, an idea of the state as embracing human life in its entirety, in which the so-called democratic majority imposes its all-inclusive will on all of the citizens without exception. This notion is completely irreconcilable with Rousseau's original idea of freedom. Absolute freedom, absolute equality, and absolute democracy do not appear to be compatible with each other.

Rousseau dissolves the idea of justice in completely formal and therefore empty categories. He does not acknowledge truly contentful principles which as such intrinsically delimit and give directions to the actions of individual men and to the various groups of society, including the state.

Rousseau's thought reveals very basic problems, with which modern social democracy, which to an important extent thinks in the same principial categories as does Rousseau, is also starkly confronted in political and social life. The way in which they

20 *Ibid.,* Book I, chapter VII.

understand social justice and the way in which they desire to realize this justice in socio-political life leads them *nolens volens* in a totalitarian direction, even without bringing the thought of Karl Marx into the picture. There is here, as I see it, an explanation of the fact that parties advocating a democratic socialism are often so intolerant of other democratic parties which do not have a typical socialistic structure. Here there comes to expression the powerful influence of socio-political principles. If one has chosen a particular principle, on whatever grounds, impelled by whatever considerations, he comes irretrievably into the grip of that principle, and that with an inner necessity.

3. Christianity

In the foregoing I have been able to draw attention only to a few aspects of ancient classical and modern thought about justice. The scope set for this article required me to observe this strict self-limitation. Nevertheless, we have already obtained in this fashion an opportunity of fixing our attention on various problems that arise when we think about justice: the origin and nature of the norms of justice, the relation of the super-arbitrary aspects of law to positive law, the role of the civil authorities in the lawmaking process, the relation of individual and community, the relation of the state to the other societal bonds that play a role in human affairs.

Along the way it will have become apparent that up to this point I have bypassed the time immediately following the ancient classical period and also the Middle Ages, and as a consequence Christian thought about justice in that time. I preferred to leave the summarization of Christian thought as a whole to one concluding section, even though there also I shall have to limit myself to discussing a number of leading ideas.

In this connection, I wish to make one preliminary observation, namely, that Christian thought too does not develop and cannot develop as a kind of *Reinkultur*. In my opinion, Dooyeweerd has correctly pointed out that, in spite of the radically different starting points of its various thinkers, we may still speak of a Western community of thought in the domain of science. To be sure, in view of all the modern developments, it is likely better to speak of a worldwide community of thought.

This is a consequence of what we indeed must call a circumstance, that Christians and non-Christians together, independent of the question whether they acknowledge it or not, are involved with each other within the framework of God's creation, which holds for all of them alike and from which no man can extricate himself. This is also true of our theoretical labors as such. No one can altogether deny this divine order without contributing to his own destruction. In this order, which is upheld in Christ, there is the only continuing basis for communication between men, including their scientific interchange.[21]

The foregoing implies that a Christian, no matter how basically he is committed, can never cut himself loose from the tradition in which he has been placed, that he can never make an altogether new beginning, isolating himself from what earlier generations, Christian or not, have left behind as the result of their cultural labors and especially as a result of their thought. In his thinking a Christian too makes continual use of the fruits of scientific labors, even as they are produced in non-Christian circles. Nevertheless, he will be called upon to handle them in a special way, directed and impelled by what the Scriptures reveal to him about creation, fall, and redemption, both in their radicality and their universality, and to integrate them in his thinking. That is to say, he will have critically to test these influences coming to him out of his tradition and to purify them from typical elements and motives of unbelief. It is indeed not a question of a radical rejection but of a reformation of the scientific enterprise.[22]

The foregoing also implies that every accomplishment of Christian thought must continually be tested as to whether it is truly Christian. In this sense too a Christian is a child of his time, in that he himself is continually subjected to the spirit of his age, even when this manifests itself to be non-Christian. As

21 See, e.g., H. Dooyeweerd, "De transcendentale critiek van het wijsgeerig denken en de grondslagen van de wijsgeerige denkgemeenschap van het Avondland," *Philosophia Reformata*, VI (1941), 1–20; "De vier religieuze grondthema's in den ontwikkelingsgang van het wijsgeerig denken van het Avondland," *Philosophia Reformata*, VI (1941), 161–179; *A New Critique of Theoretical Thought*, I (Amsterdam: H. J. Paris, and Philadelphia: Presbyterian and Reformed, 1953), part I, chapter I.

22 Dooyeweerd, *A New Critique*, I, 117.

a consequence of the situation in which he lives, broken as it is by sin, and as a consequence of the brokenness of his own existence, no Christian can completely escape the influence of the spirit of the time, not even in his theoretical thought. There does not exist anything such as a pure reason, a pure rationality, that could correct itself in its own power, in conformity with the rules of logic. Every act of thought — and scientific activity is no exception to the rule — is a completely human activity, in which man is involved with his entire personality, with all the consequences thereof. There does not exist any free-standing thought.[23] Neither is the present generation excluded from this stricture. Those that follow will, in turn, have to test the accomplishments of present-day Christian thought in the light of what the Bible teaches us concerning creation, fall, and redemption.

The foregoing, therefore, involves a multiple relativizing of Christian thought and its results. This thought is relative, in the first place, because all of its results have no more than a provisional, a mixed character, and as such must be evaluated continually. Christian thought is also relative, in the second place, because it, just as all other forms of thought, is not self-sufficient, is not autonomous, but participates in what Dooyeweerd has called the meaning character of reality. Theoretical thought cannot be exercised apart from human personality and cannot be carried on, furthermore, in a meaningful way in isolation from what those who, renewed in Christ as Creator and Lord as well as Redeemer, have brought us to know about reality as it is given to us, that is to say, apart from the Triune God, in Whom man consists, even with respect to his scientific thought. Might I refer back at this point to what I said before concerning the real validity of the order of creation, for Christians as well as non-Christians?[24] It is in this spirit that I hope to continue my discussion.

*

[23] Attention is called to a paper written by the author of this article, which will soon appear in *Philosophia Reformata* with the title "Ontisch en/of intentioneel? Een bijdrage tot de discussie inzake de aard en structuur van het wetenschappelijk denken binnen de reformatorische wijsbegeerte."

[24] Cf. Dooyeweerd, *A New Critique,* I, 4, 101.

It can be established in a very general sense, that wherever there is talk among Christian thinkers about the idea of justice with respect to earthly relationships, this takes place for the most part in relation to the idea of a divine or created order.

*

Karl Barth, however, undoubtedly qualifies as an exception in this respect.

Barth acknowledges unambiguously, that, for instance, the state (referred to by him as *"Bürgergemeinde*) no less than the church (referred to by him as *Christengemeinde*) is a divine institution: "Knowing that, it [namely, the Christian church] recognizes in the existence of the civil community — disregarding the Christianity or lack of Christianity of its members and officials and also disregarding the particular forms which it assumes — no less than in its own existence, the operation of a divine ordinance (*ordinatio,* i.e., institution or foundation), an *exousia* which is and acts in accordance with the will of God (Romans 13: 1 f.). However much human error and human tyranny may be involved in it, the State is not a product of sin but one of the constants of the divine Providence and government of the world in its action against human sin: it is therefore an instrument of divine grace. The civil community shares both a common origin and a common centre with the Christian community. It is an order of divine grace inasmuch as in relation to sinful man as such, in relation to the world that still needs redeeming, the *grace* of God is always the *patience* of God. It is the sign that mankind, in its total ignorance and darkness, which is still, or has again become, a prey to sin and therefore subject to the wrath of God, is not yet forsaken but preserved and sustained by God. It serves to protect man from the invasion of *chaos* and therefore to give him time: time for the preaching of the gospel; time for repentance; time for faith."[25] The state as

---

[25] Karl Barth, "The Christian Community and the Civil Community," taken up in *Community, State, and Church: Three Essays* (Gloucester, Mass.: Peter Smith, 1968), pp. 149–189; quote from pp. 155–156. Original German: "Indem sie das weiss, erkennt sie in der Existenz der Bürgergemeinde — ohne Rücksicht auf das Christentum oder Nicht-Christentum ihrer Angehörigen und Funktionäre und auch ohne Rücksicht auf ihre besondere Gestalt und Wirklichkeit — nicht weniger als in ihrer eigenen

a particular divine ordinance is for that reason not related here in any fashion whatever to the original creation; it falls entirely within the sphere of the church, of the congregation, as a sign of God's redeeming grace. The meaning of community in the body politic is securing the external, relative, provisional freedom of the individual as well as the external, relative, provisional peace of this community, the guarantor of the external, relative, provisional humanity. The civil community is, for this reason, an external institute that embraces both believers and unbelievers and concerning which no one can make a direct appeal to God's Word and Spirit. As such it is spiritually blind and naive. It has neither faith, nor love, nor hope.[26]

Barth, therefore, will not accept that the state is a creature of God that is related in a direct sense religiously to God as its creator. Although it has been ordained by God, the state remains a neutral instrument to withstand the chaos in the world, in order to make possible the life of the church community in the world. Therefore, for the state tolerance in religious matters is the ultimate wisdom.[27]

Barth's view of the state is founded undoubtedly in his Christomonism, in which creation and recreation (redemption) are not seen as two independent acts of God, but which com-

Existenz die Auswirkung einer göttlichen Anordnung (ordinatio, Einsetzung, Stiftung), eine exousia, die nicht ohne, sondern nach Gottes Willen ist und wirksame ist (Röm. 13:1b). Wo Bürgergemeinde, wo Staat ist, da haben wir es . . . mit einer der Konstanten der göttlichen Vorsehung und Weltregierung in ihrer zugunsten des Menschen stattfindenden Gegenwirkung gegen die menschliche Sünde und also mit einem Instrument der göttlichen Gnade zu tun. Die Bürgergemeinde hat mit der Christengemeinde sowohl den Ursprung als auch das Zentrum gemeinsam. Sie ist Ordnung der göttlichen *Gnade,* sofern diese immer auch *Geduld* ist. Sie ist das Zeichen dafür, dass auch die noch (oder schon wider) der Sünde und also dem Zorn verfallene Menschheit in ihrer ganzen Unwissenheit und Lichtlosigkeit von Gott nicht verlassen, sondern bewahrt und gehalten ist. Sie dient ja dazu, den Menschen vor dem Einbruch des *Chaos* zu schützen und also ihm Zeit zu geben: Zeit für die Verkündigung des Evangeliums, Zeit zur Busse, Zeit zum Glauben." *Christengemeinde und Bürgergemeinde* (Bielefeld: Ludwig Bechaufverlag, n.d.), pp. 12–13. The form of the quote is taken from the edition of 1946 (Zollikon-Zürich: Evangelischer Verlag), pp. 9–10.

[26] Barth, *op cit.,* p. 151.

[27] *Ibid.*

pletely coalesce. Or, as Barth himself expresses it: "The world came into being, it was created and sustained *by the little child that was born in Bethlehem, by the Man who died on the Cross of Golgotha, and the third day rose again.*"[28] (Italics mine.)

In light of the foregoing, it is also understandable that Barth says that the true law of the church is an example to "worldly" law, "For all its particularity, it is a pattern for the formation and administration of human law generally, and therefore of the law of other political, economic, cultural and other human societies."[29]

*

We come across similar thoughts in the French jurist and sociologist Jacques Ellul, who has been strongly influenced by Barth and who has become known especially during the last decade in the Anglo-Saxon world. We find these thoughts especially in his little book published in 1946, *The Theological Foundation of Law.*[30]

[28] Karl Barth, *Dogmatics in Outline* (London: SCM, 1949), p. 58. Original German: "Die Welt wurde, sie ist geschaffen und getragen durch das Kindlein, das zu Bethlehem geboren wurde, durch den Mann, der am Kreuz von Golgatha gestorben und am dritten Tage wieder auferstanden ist." *Dogmatik im Grundriss* (Zollikon-Zürich: Evangelischer Verlag, 1947), p. 66. For a treatment of Barth's doctrine of creation, see also Dion. Kempff, *Die skeppingsleer van Karl Barth* (Amsterdam-Kaapstad-Pretoria, 1949) and S. U. Zuidema, "The Structure of Karl Barth's Doctrine of Creation," *Communication and Confrontation: A Philosophical Appraisal and Critique of Modern Society and Contemporary Thought* (Assen: Royal Van Gorcum and Kampen: J. H. Kok, 1974), pp. 309–328.

[29] Karl Barth, *Church Dogmatics*, IV, 2 (Edinburgh: T. and T. Clark, 1958), p. 719. Original German: ". . . in seiner ganzen Eigenartigkeit exemplarisch für die Bildung und Handhabung des menschlichen Rechtes überhaupt und also des Rechtes auch der anderen, der politischen, wirtschaftlichen, kulturellen und sonstigen menschlichen Gemeinschaften." *Kirchliche Dogmatik*, IV, 2 (Zollikon-Zürich: Evangelischer Verlag, 1955), p. 815. Quoted by Hommes, *Hoofdlijnen*, p. 298.

[30] Jacques Ellul, *The Theological Foundation of Law* (New York: Seabury, 1969). Tr. from the French, *Le fondement théologique du droit* (Neuchatel and Paris: Delachaux & Niestlé, 1946). For a more extensive treatment of the thought of Ellul, see J. D. Dengerink, "Das Wort Gottes und die zeitlichen sozialen Ordnungen: Eine Betrachtung zum heutigen reformierten Denken," *Philosophia Reformata*, XX (1955), 97–122. This

In Ellul's thought we discover to a limited extent the doctrine of the creation ordinances, in particular when he deals with institutions such as marriage and the state. He describes these institutions as creations of God, in the same sense that trees and light, man and the angels are created. According to him these institutions, as creations of God, have their foundation solely in Jesus Christ. They possess no significance of their own apart from the incarnation and from redemption. In that incarnation and that redemption they have their ultimate cause as well as their goal. They have meaning only as they participate in this work of salvation. Man therefore cannot dispose over these institutions in his own strength. Even though they are changeable as to their form, their reality always remains the same. Man does not have to discover and form them — because they are (*elles sont*); man only needs to use them (*à les utiliser*). They do not serve him as examples or models; instead, he lives out of them (*il en vit*).[31]

This thought about the existence of super-arbitrary creation ordinances is mingled in Ellul, however, with a completely different view of justice, one that stands at right angles to the idea of creation ordinances. That is apparent especially when Ellul begins to speak of divine justice.[32]

Divine justice is characterized in the first place as being an expression of God's transcendence. As such it is a sign of the judgment that will come at the end of time (*comme le signe du jugement de la terre à la fin des temps*). The various aspects of this divine righteousness find their deeper unity in the person of Jesus Christ, who has been made righteousness for us. There is no righteousness, therefore, not even of a relative kind, outside of him. There is no righteousness at all independently of God. What is righteous is whatever is conformable to God's will. Furthermore, we may not understand this righteousness as something static, as an objective right in terms of which everyone is judged in his situation. We know the will of God only from his revelation, that is to say, from God's act, here and now. The

article has been published in abridged form in *The Gordon Review*, XI (1969), 191–204, with the title "The Word of God and the Temporal Structures of Society."

[31] Ellul, *op. cit.*, pp. 76ff.

[32] *Ibid.*, pp. 37ff.

will of God is not a principle from which we could deduce basic propositions; it is always a divine act (*elle est toujours acte*). And this judging activity takes place always within the context of the covenant, in which God binds the course of life to particular preconditions.

Within the covenant, therefore, right is not a system for organizing society. Instead, it is a precondition of life that is imposed on man. A man, therefore, cannot assert that he has an enduring claim to certain rights. In essence human rights are contingent and changeable. Their content depends upon the historical circumstances. Every society desires to construct a law system of its own. Indeed, one immediately recognizes a right that is properly his. He is, however, not in a position to grasp this right objectively (*de reconnaître objectivement le Droit, ou encore les droits de l'humanité*).[33]

The sole task given to man is to earn his living and to preserve the species. For this purpose he has received the necessary means, i.e., specialized understanding, hands, eyes, etc. He does not know, however, what is right in society; he knows only that he must act, order, judge, etc. In this domain he is, as in all others, completely a "homo faber." By means of his understanding he has the possibility of developing a completely relative, purely pragmatic, temporary criterion of righteousness. Man does not conform to an ideal but strives after a practical result.

In Ellul's thought we are faced with the situation that, on the one hand, the biblical creation motif is certainly present, and yet, on the other hand, it is possible to establish, according to him, only in a very fragmentary fashion what this creation order is. There are only fragments remaining of the order of creation, such as the institutions to which he refers, marriage and the state. For that matter, the order of creation does not include life in its fullness. There is a broad area left over to human inventiveness, in the domain of jurisprudence. The institutions in question are nothing more than established survey points, out from which society should be built.

According to Ellul, therefore, human law has a two-fold task. In the first place, it must give to the institutions that have their foundation in creation a concrete form. In the second place, it

33 *Ibid.*, pp. 81 ff.

has the task of filling in the gaps observed between the institutions (*combler le vide entre les institutions voulues par Dieu*). It is also true, indeed, of the divine institutions that they possess a kind of permanency; but they do not have a criterion belonging to them by means of which we might connect them with the life and order before the fall.[34]

In this way the biblical motif of creation is pushed farther and farther back in Ellul's thought, in order to make room for an activistic and actualistic pragmatism, in which there is no longer a place for enduring principles founded in the order of creation. In important areas of legal praxis we are threatened with being swept away in the currents of history. The "agir" and "organiser" of which Ellul speaks appear very much like the hopeless struggles of a drowning man, who can find no solid ground under his feet.

*

The thought of Barth and Ellul is, however, uncharacteristic of Christian thought about justice through the ages. One can place their voluntarism in the line of nominalism, as that arose particularly in the high Middle Ages within the Christian church and with which especially the name of William of Ockham is connected.

Going back much farther, we come across another line of thought, in addition, in which the biblical ideas of creation and the order of creation are taken into account with much greater force and consistency. In this connection it is especially Augustine who comes to mind.

*

At the heart of Augustine's thought is the belief in the absolute sovereignty of the God of creation. According to him, therefore, we should not attempt to peer behind God's sovereign Creator-will: "For if the will of God has a cause, there is something that precedes the will of God, which is wicked to believe. To one therefore, who asks, 'Why did God make heaven and earth?' the answer should be given, 'Because he wanted to.' For the will of God is the cause of heaven and earth, and for

---

[34] *Ibid.,* pp. 107–108.

that reason the will of God is higher than heaven and earth. Whoever then asks, why he willed to make heaven and earth, asks about something greater than the will of God, nothing greater than which can be discovered."[35] And elsewhere Augustine writes: "He who aims to discover God's design in the creation of the world is seeking the motive of God's will. Now every cause is productive of some effect. Moreover every efficient cause is greater than its effect. But nothing is greater than the will of God. Therefore we must not seek its motive."[36]

Augustine stoutly adheres to the belief that the creation of the entire world of which man is a part is a creation out of nothing (*creatio ex nihilo*): "Nor had you any material in your hand when you were making heaven and earth: for where should you have got what you had not yet made to use as material? What exists, save because you exist? You spoke and heaven and earth were created; in your word you created them."[37] Even matter is a creation of God: "Thus, Lord, you created the world out of formless matter: and it was of nothing that you created this almost-nothing, out of which you have made the mighty things which we children of men marvel at."[38] Augustine clearly rejects

[35] "Si enim habet causam voluntas Dei, est aliquid quod antecedat voluntatem Dei, quod nefas est credere. Qui ergo dicit: quare fecit Deus caelum et terram? respondendum est ei: quia voluit. Voluntas enim Dei causa est caeli et terrae, et ideo major est voluntas Dei quam caelum et terra. Qui autem dicit: quare voluit facere caelum et terram, majus aliquid quaerit quam est voluntas Dei: nihil autem majus inveniri potest." Augustine, *De Genesi contra Manichaeos*, 1, 2, 4, cited by Etienne Gilson: *The Christian Philosophy of Saint Augustine* (New York: Random House, 1960), notes to Part III, chapter I, note 16; pp. 336–337. Tr. from the French, *Introduction à l'étude de Saint Augustin* (2nd ed., Paris: J. Vrin, 1943; quoted from 4th ed., 1969).

[36] "Qui quaerit quare voluerit Deus mundum facere, causam quaerit voluntatis Dei. Sed omnis causa efficiens est. Omne autem efficiens majus est quam id quod efficitur. Nihil autem majus est voluntate Dei. Non ergo ejus causa quaerenda est." Augustine, *De diversis quaestionibus 83, quaes.* 28; cited by Gilson, *op. cit.*, p. 337.

[37] "Nec manu tenebas aliquid, unde faceres caelum et terram: nam unde tibi hoc, quod tu non feceras, unde aliquid faceres? quid enim est, nisi quia tu es? ergo dixisti et facta sunt atque in uerbo tuo fecisti ea." Augustine, *Confessiones*, XI, 5; cf. XI, 6. Cf. Gilson, *op. cit.*, p. 341.

[38] "Tu enim, domine, fecisti mundum de materia informi, quam fecisti de nulla re paene nullam rem, unde faceres magna, quae miramur filii hominum." Augustine, *Confessiones*, XII, 8.

the idea of emanation: ". . . the Self-same, Holy, Holy, Holy, Lord God Almighty — you, Lord, in the beginning, which is from you, in your wisdom, which is born of your substance, made something and made it *of nothing*. You created heaven and earth, but *not of your own substance:* for in that event they would have been equal to your only-begotten Son and hence to yourself; and it would have been altogether unjust that something not proceeding from you should be equal to you. But, apart from you there was no other thing existent to make them of, O God, Trinity that is One, Unity that is Three. Therefore it was *of nothing* that you made heaven and earth, the great thing and the small thing: for you are almighty and good and must make all things good, the great heaven and the small earth."[39] (Italics mine.) Therefore the act of creation too falls outside of time, because time is also a creation of God: "How could countless ages pass when you, the Author and Creator of all ages, had not yet made them? What time could there be that you had not created? . . . If there was time, you made it, for time could not pass before you made time."[40]

There is a direct connection between Augustine's belief in creation and his thought that in the world we have to do with an ordered, a structured reality. In the world there is the expression of a set pattern. Augustine proceeds from the thought that the understanding as to its nature is so constructed, that according to the order of nature, by reason of the divine providence of the Creator, it is subjected to "res intelligibiles." These are, Gilson says, none other than the divine ideas themselves,

---

[39] ". . . et id ipsum, sanctus, sanctus, sanctus, dominus deus omnipotens, in principio, quod est de te, in sapientia tua, quae nata est de substantia tua, fecisti aliquid et de nihilo. fecisti enim caelum et terram non de te: nam esset aequale unigenito tuo, ac per hoc et tibi, et nullo modo iustum esset, ut aequale tibi esset, quod de te non esset. et aliud praeter te non erat, unde faceres ea, deus, uns trinitas et trina unitas: et ideo de nihilo fecisti caelum et terram, magnum quiddam et paruum quiddam, quoniam omnipotens et bonus es ad facienda omnia bona, magnum caelum et paruum terram." Augustine, *Confessiones,* XII, 7.

[40] "Nam unde poterant innumerabilia saecula praeterire, quae ipse non feceras, cum sis omnium saeculorum auctor et conditor? aut quae tempora fuissent, quae abs te condita non essent? . . . Id ipsum enim tempus tu feceras, nec praeterire potuerunt tempora, antequam faceres tempora." Augustine, *Confessiones,* XI, 13.

which are referred to by Augustine with various names, such as *ideae, formae, species, rationes,* or *regulae.* In this Augustine draws from Plato, with this principial difference, however, that for Augustine the ideas do not together form a world or a reality that is self-sufficient, but are instead embraced in divine thought (*in divina intelligentia continentur*). Nevertheless, along with Plato he assumes that these ideas, just because they are contained in the divine reason, are eternal, unchangeable, and as such unformed, having no beginning or end. Instead, they are the archetypes of every kind and of every individual created by God, the model according to which each thing is created. Because the ideas can exist only in God's thought, they do not belong either to created reality, they are not concreated with subjective (i.e., subjected to the ideas), factual existence. "For ideas are certain original images of determined and unchangeable causes of things and for this reason they are eternal, permanent and ever encompassed by the divine intelligence. And as they have neither beginning nor end, they act as the type according to which is fashioned everything that can begin and end, everything that can appear and disappear," as Augustine writes in his *Concerning Various Questions.*[41]

It is clear that, with this line of thought, Augustine establishes a tension in principle between the eternal and unchangeable ideas and created reality, which is as such subject in principle to change. He thus carries with him some of the problems connected with the Platonic legacy.

Furthermore, Augustine connects this doctrine of the creation ordinances, which stands under the influence of Plato, with the Stoic conception of the *logoi spermatikoi,* the teaching that every man carries with him a spark of the world reason. This is the case, insofar as in Augustine the creation ideas also function

---

[41] "Sunt namque ideae principales formae quaedam, vel rationes rerum stabiles atque incommutabiles, quae ipsae formatae non sunt, ac per hoc aeternae ac semper eodem modo se habentes, quae in divina intelligentia continentur. Et cum ipsae neque oriantur, neque intereant, secundum eas tamen formari dicitur omne quod oriri et interire potest, et omne quod oritur et interit." Augustine, *De diversis quaestionibus 83,* quaes. 46,2; cited by Gilson, *op. cit.,* p. 291. Also see Etienne Gilson, *The Spirit of Medieval Philosophy* (New York: Charles Scribners Sons, 1936), pp. 154ff.

as individuated forms of being (*rationes seminales*). The eternal law (*lex aetêrna*) is imprinted as a law of nature (*lex naturalis*) in the human soul, so that human life might be a mirroring of the divine guidance of the world.[42] Elsewhere Augustine speaks of the ideas, which the mind "can see with its inner, intelligible eye."[43] Natural justice is viewed therefore as a copy of the eternal idea of justice in the human soul, as "a disposition of the soul, respecting the general welfare, to render to each his due according to his station."[44]

Referring to Joh. Sauter, *The Philosophical Foundations of Natural Law* (1932)[45] and Michel Villey, *The Formation of Modern Juridical Thought* (1968),[46] Hommes remarks that Augustine's conception of positive law is not very consistent. In view of some passages the conclusion can be drawn that all positive law must be founded in natural law (i.e., therefore, the divine ideas) in order to have the force of law. There are, on the contrary, other passages from which one might conclude that legal force attaches to all positive law, irrespective of its content.[47] What is important about Augustine's thought is, however, that in spite of all the other influences we think we see in it the biblical idea of creation stands at its center. Thereby Augustine made a contribution of incalculable value to Christian thought about justice.

*

Gilson has repeatedly pointed out, that neither Plato nor Aristotle had a veritable idea of creation, and that this holds

---

[42] Augustine, *De diversis quaestionibus 83,* quaes. 53,2. Cf. Hommes, *Hoofdlijnen,* p. 39.

[43] "intueri posse . . . oculo suo interiore atque intelligibili." Augustine, *De diversis quaestionibus 83,* quaes. 46,2; cited by Gilson, *The Christian Philosophy of St. Augustine,* p. 291.

[44] "habitus animi, communi utilitate conservata, suam cuique tribuens dignitatem." Augustine, *De diversis quaestionibus 83,* quaes. 31. Cf. Hommes, *Hoofdlijnen,* p. 39.

[45] Joh. Sauter, *Die philosophischen Grundlagen des Naturrechts: Untersuchungen zur Geschichte der Rechts- und Staatslehre* (Vienna, 1932, 2nd ed.; Frankfurt: Sauer and Auvermann, 1966).

[46] Michel Villey, *La formation de la pensée juridique moderne: Cours d'histoire de la philosophie du droit, 1961–1966* (Paris: Montchrestien, 1968).

[47] Hommes, *Hoofdlijnen,* p. 39.

for the thought of classical antiquity as a whole.[48] On the contrary, the idea of creation and the idea of providence connected with it continually play, according to him, a central role in Christian thought, in particular, that of the Middle Ages.

Gilson also makes the global remark that, in making the transition from Platonism to Holy Scripture, one is immediately struck by the fact that instead of having to do with a number of artisans who once and for all have bound themselves in their work to certain rules, he finds himself in the presence of a God who, once he has created the world, holds it in his hands (*le possède*). And he holds fast to it jealously. Jahwe does not cease to declare his right of authorship and constantly to remind the world of it. And the Bible continually bases on this right the prerogative (*pouvoir*) of God to guide human affairs according to his will. It is the omnipotence of God, as that is revealed in his works, that also gives him the prerogative of establishing what will remain even in the Gospel the first and great commandment, You shall love your God, and you shall serve him with all your heart and with all your soul. This God, to whom everything belongs, is also the God whom nothing escapes. Man does not depend therefore, as in the philosophy of Plato, on an impersonal law but on a person upon whose will depend his existence and his destiny.[49]

This makes it understandable, according to Gilson, why the first Christian thinkers were so inclined to emphasize the notion of providence as one of the characteristic traits of the new conception of the universe. Both the Stoic conception of fate and the Stoic idea of indifference were dead. The mechanical world of Lucretius and Democritus made way for a cosmos of which every element was chosen, created, and predestined with love. Divine providence takes on a new dimension. The personal relations that bind each creature to his Creator extend to all of nature. The pure thought of Aristotle, which shares its eternity with a universe it has not created and does not know, is replaced with the Heavenly Father, whose creative benevolence extends to the smallest blade of grass.[50]

*

[48] Gilson, *The Spirit of Medieval Philosophy*, pp. 69, 76, 156–158, 243, 268.
[49] *Ibid.*, pp. 151–153.
[50] *Ibid.*, pp. 153–155.

The best historical witnesses of Christian thought, according to Gilson, have seen very clearly that the idea of creation is the true foundation (*le fondement ultime*) of Christian providence. In this connection Gilson points to Athenagoras and Irenaeus. Thomas Aquinas too is placed by Gilson in this tradition. God is the first and completely perfect being, which as such must of necessity be the cause of everything that exists. There is no pre-existing matter. Everything is included in the act of creation, even including matter. The causal relations in nature also do not exist apart from the prior causal relation between the Creator and nature. "For he [Aristotle] proves in *Metaphysics*, II, that that which is most true and most being is the cause of being for all existing things. Hence it follows that the very being in potency which primary matter has is derived from the first principle of being, which is the most being. Therefore, it is not necessary to presuppose something for its action which has not been produced by it."[51]

It is not possible to proceed to infinity in the series of efficient causes and of moved things, for then there would be no prime mover. Thus there must be a first mover, who himself is not moved by anything else, and who is God. As Creator, God is the prime initiator of movement.[52] God, therefore, is the beginning as well as the goal of all things. As such he is altogether self-sufficient. "God, by His providence, directs all things to His goodness as their end: not indeed as though His goodness gained any thing from the things that are made, but in order that the likeness of His goodness may be impressed on things as far as possible."[53]

Gilson avers that all Christian thinkers in the Middle Ages,

[51] "Probat enim in II Metaphys., quod id quod est maxime verum et maxime ens, est causa essendi omnibus existentibus: unde hoc ipsum esse in potentia, quod habet materia prima, sequitur derivatum esse a primo essendi principio, quod est maxima ens. Non igitur necesse est praesupponi aliquid ejus actioni, quod non sit ab eo productum." Thomas Aquinas, *In Phys.*, lib. VIII, lect. 2, art. 4; cited by Gilson, *op. cit.*, p. 441.

[52] Gilson, *op. cit.*, pp. 75–77.

[53] "Deus per suam providentiam omnia ordinat in divinam bonitatem sicut in finem; non autem hoc modo quod suae bonitati aliquid per ea quae fiunt, accrescat, sed ut similitudo suae bonitatis, quantum possibile est, imprimatur in rebus." Thomas Aquinas, *Summa Contra Gentiles*, III, 97; cited by Gilson, *op. cit.*, p. 163; cf. p. 158.

furthermore, agree with Augustine when they assert the existence of ideas and claim that the knowledge of these ideas is the heart of philosophy, even though they do not all conceive of these ideas in the same way. Like Augustine, Thomas Aquinas is of the opinion that the ideas are *in* God and that they are the forms according to whose likeness things are made. They belong as such to the essence of God. They are what is communicable in that essence. The concept "idea," furthermore, has no meaning other than in relation to a possible creation. There are no ideas in God that are not conformable to concrete existence. In this regard, Gilson remarks, the ideas as conceived by Thomas differ clearly from those as conceived by Plato. For the latter the ideas would continue in existence, even though there should be no real world, for just because they are the highest reality, these intelligible essences are self-sufficient. They have no relation other than to themselves; they have their goal in themselves. In Thomas, even as in Augustine, Bonaventure, and Duns Scotus, on the contrary, it is only the divine essence itself that has relation to itself. An idea, on the contrary, has meaning only in connection with the possibility of a creation and as an expression of the relation of possible creations to the creating essence. This explains why everything that exists has its idea in the Essence from which it derives its existence, that there are ideas in God of the individuals themselves and indeed preeminently of the individuals, because they are truly real and because in the individuals the species exist. According to Thomas, the idea is in essence the knowledge that God has of his own essence, in so far as this essence is communicable.[54]

The ideas, even though they participate in the divine essence, have an inner connection with individual things, to what is particular. What is particular, however, is, in its turn, inseparable from its order. "Now individuals are beings, and more so than universals: because universals do not exist by themselves, but only in individuals. Therefore divine providence is concerned about individuals also."[55] But, on the contrary what is particu-

---

[54] Gilson, *op. cit.*, pp. 156–159.

[55] "Singularia autem sunt entia, et magis quam universalia, quia universalia non subsistunt per se, sed sunt solum in singularibus. Est igitur divina providentia etiam singularium." Thomas, *Summa contra gentiles,* III, 75; cited by Gilson, *op. cit.*, p. 461.

lar is inseparable from its order. The order of a work is part of the work.[56] Gilson concludes, that if there are indeed intellectual acts of knowing, their cause cannot be an abstract principle such as thought in general; it has to be of necessity a principle that is concrete and real and for that reason exists in a particular nature. Wherever there are acts of thought, therefore, there are thinking substances.[57]

The foregoing implies, therefore, that every thing has its own destiny. Out of his superabundant perfection God communicates being to everything that exists. He does not do that because of a necessity of nature but through a decision of will. God is Lord, therefore, over his works, even as we are lord over our works. But if things have been brought forth by an active will, each one of them has a particular goal. Every thing attains its ultimate goal by means of its activity; but this action must be directed by Him who himself gave to things the possibilities through which they can act. Nothing is excepted from God's government, just as there is nothing that does not derive its existence from him.[58]

In this connection it is good to remember that Thomas does not assert only that the aforementioned ideas are simply in God; more precisely, they have their place in divine thought.[59] With reference to "natural reality" in general, for that matter, it is the case for Thomas that it is the product of God as the creative logos. As such both the creation and the ideas of creation are rational in character and as a consequence are rationally understandable. In his thought within the domain of nature man does not require per se the enlightenment of divine revelation. Understood in that sense, both the creation and human thought about (the structure of) the creation possess a relative autonomy with reference to the supernatural kingdom of grace, as this is embodied particularly in the institution of the church.[60]

---

[56] Gilson, *op. cit.*, p. 161.
[57] *Ibid.*, p. 184.
[58] *Ibid.*, p. 165.
[59] *Ibid.*, pp. 160–161.
[60] On this point see in particular H. Dooyeweerd, "De idee der individualiteits-structuur en het thomistisch substantiebegrip: Een critisch onderzoek naar de grondslagen der thomistische zijnsleer," *Philosophia Reformata*, VIII (1943), 65–99; IX (1944), 1–41; X (1945), 25–48; XI

In Thomas' thought we have to do, therefore, with an all-inclusive order, which has its original locus in divine thought, the divine logos. This order, therefore, participates in the divine essence; but at the same time it penetrates in a real way all individual things, insofar as the divine ideas operate as forming principles in individual things.

Within the framework of this rationalistically conceived rational-ethical order of the world (natural) law also has its place. In the line of Plato and Aristotle, Thomas views law as the object of moral virtue of justice, i.e., the continuing inclination of the will to render to each his due.

Taken in a broad sense, justice is the all-embracing term to designate the totality of virtues or moral perfection. Whoever gives to each his due (to God what is due him; to one's neighbor what is due him) fulfills the sum of moral obligations. In a narrower sense, justice is a particular duty besides those of wisdom, moderation, and courage. Justice is then the virtue that renders to each his due in a strict sense, i.e., what is rightly his. Taken in this sense, justice never refers to the act itself, but to others.

What is his own (*suum*) in a strict sense is more precisely formulated by Thomas in line with his teleological thought as that which is dispensed to someone as a means of coming to his own perfection. Under this rubric is included not only one's relationship to external objects but also that which pertains to authentic human personality.

In addition, Thomas makes a clear distinction between commutative justice (*justitia commutativa*) and distributive justice (*justitia distributiva*). The former, namely, has to do with mutual intercourse between individuals (individual entities), in which they stand beside each other as equals, and are therefore not taken up in some communal bond. In such a situation there is an unqualified *quid pro quo*. Thomas refers, in this connection, by way of illustration, to the relation between individuals originating in a contractual arrangement. Distributive justice, on the contrary, has to do with relationships within a community.

(1946), 22–52; and H. Dooyeweerd, "De leer der analogie in de thomistische wijsbegeerte en in de wijsbegeerte der wetsidee," *Philosophia Reformata*, VII (1942), 47–57.

Here those who are charged with administering the law take into account the position which those who are involved have within the community. That is to say, in terms of the distributive justice pertaining here, rights and obligations (duties) can be distributed unequally, in part depending on the ability of the individual members to bear them: equal treatment of equals and unequal treatment of unequals.[61]

As a third type of justice Thomas cites legal justice (*justitia legalis*), justice before the law. Here, by means of the law, is determined what devolves upon each member of the state to contribute to the whole. Legal justice, together with distributive justice, comprises the terrain of public justice.

As Thomas turns to describe these three forms of justice more narrowly in teleological terms, he asserts the following:

    a. that commutative justice has as its end protecting the mutual freedom and independence of the individuals;
    b. that legal justice has as its end guaranteeing the existence and the prosperity of the body politic;
    c. that distributive justice has as its end protecting the members of the community in their rights relative to the community.

These various forms of law have their objective foundation in so-called natural law, i.e., a body of norms which does not derive its validity from any positive declaration, whether by God (e.g., the ceremonial law given by Moses), or by man, but which derives its validity from the universally valid natural law (*lex naturalis*) itself, a natural law that can be derived, apart from all revelation, by direct or indirect deductions from the basic ethical principle "Do good and avoid evil."

This natural law is so immediately evident, be it only in its general basic principles, that it can count on being recognized by all men. Positive law is required in order to make further deductions and for making more precise determinations (i.e., such as are not derivable from the moral law of nature) in connection with the changing circumstances of time and place. The latter, furthermore, is necessary to provide appropriate sanctions for the rules of the law of nature. Positive law remains,

---

[61] Cf. Thomas Aquinas, *Summa Theologica*, I, 21; cf. also H. Dooyeweerd, *Encyclopaedie der rechtswetenschap*, I, 146ff.

however, completely dependent here upon natural law. That is, every actual provision of the law that is in conflict with natural law is not binding.

Objective natural law embraces, therefore, only general principles of natural law together with the provisions that can be immediately deduced from it. Thomas then does not acknowledge any changeable legal principles founded in the course of history, *but only a timeless, unchangeable natural law*.[62]

The latter is a direct consequence of Thomas' conception that the moral ideas and therefore also the principles of natural law as a part of the divine moral law have their place *in* the thought of God as the creative logos, as the first, itself unmoved and unchangeable mover of the universe in its hierarchical structure. The logos speculation, which is un-Christian in its origins, concerning the "essence" of God appears to have a rigidifying effect on the thought of Thomas concerning positive law and concerning justice, with the result that he cannot arrive at a truly internally consistent idea of either of them.

*

In concluding this historical overview, I wish to call attention to still one more thinker, because in him we discover both the actualistic line of Barth and Ellul and the traditional natural law doctrine as we encountered it in Augustine and Thomas. I refer, namely, to Emil Brunner. Since I have already presented elsewhere an extensive treatment of Brunner's thought on this score, I shall limit myself here to describing certain major lines of his position.[63]

Brunner maintains that the world is not a chaos, to which we give form. The world is already formed, and we must adapt ourselves to its order. This holds for both nature and history. It belongs to our existence, which is created by God and yet sinful,

---

[62] Cf. Dooyeweerd, *op. cit.*, pp. 143ff.

[63] Cf. J. D. Dengerink, "Enkele aspecten van het begrip 'orde' bij Emil Brunner," *Rechtsgeleerde opstellen: Door zijn leerlingen aangeboden aan prof. Dr. H. Dooyeweerd ter gelegenheid van zijn 25-jarig hoogleraarschap aan de Vrije Universiteit* (Kampen: J. H. Kok, 1951), pp. 203–220; and Dengerink, "Das Wort Gottes und die zeitlichen sozialen Ordnungen: Eine Betrachtung zum heutigen reformierten Denken," *Philosophia Reformata*, XX (1955), 97–122, as well as this article in abridged form in *The Gordon Review*, XI (1969), 191–204.

that this order is incorporated in all kinds of ordinances, such as natural laws, customs, mores, and usages. Brunner's general designation for this phenomenon is "law" (*lex*). Without this "law," life cannot go on.[64]

Brunner then emphasizes that this order may not be viewed as something that is given simply as a matter of fact, for God as the Creator is the only true Lord of our existence and of this world. Therefore, we owe respect to everything that exists. We must listen to the will of God, which speaks to us in reality. The ordinances in question are not, to be sure, *necessities* of life presented to our understanding; they are a *possibility* of life given us by God. That one come to terms with the existing order is, therefore, the first commandment of Christian ethics, even though, as it will yet become clear, it is not the ultimate one. The "law" is not identical with God's commandment but clearly stands under God's commandment.[65]

At that, Brunner is concerned not only with the will of God, as this is present immanently in existing reality. There is not only an intrinsic order *of* social life; there are also ordinances *for* social life. There is a norm that transcends all human laws, agreements, mores, and customs, an order that as such is the product of God's will. God is not an immanent logos, but the lawgiver of the world. There are *creation ordinances,* which as unchangeable preconditions — we might say, transcendental presuppositions — underlie the entire course of history. In their actual configuration they are subject to change; in their fundamental structure they are not. Brunner speaks here of *creaturely constants,* which are understood by the Christian faith as ordinances of the Creator.[66]

This idea of creation ordinances is relativized by Brunner in two ways.

According to him, the relativity of the creation ordinances is manifest, in the first place, in concrete historical reality. All thought about justice, he says — and here we see a problematic

[64] Emil Brunner, *The Divine Imperative* (Philadelphia: Westminster Press, 1947,), pp. 124–125, 140ff., 220–221.

[65] *Ibid.,* pp. 123ff., 142f., 213–214.

[66] Emil Brunner, *Justice and the Social Order* (New York and London: Harper, 1945), pp. 18f., 33, 46ff., 73f., 83, 96. Brunner, *The Divine Imperative,* pp. 210, 337.

arise that has burdened Western thought as a whole from ancient times to the present — that takes as its point of reference the divine law is as to its nature *static*. This staticness, however, is in sharp contrast to the *dynamic* of history. What yesterday was just can today be even scandalously unjust. With life's changes justice must also change. The world into which justice must introduce its order is, namely, the world not only as it is created by God but also as it is alienated.

There is, therefore, a two-fold justice:

In the first place, there is that which is just of itself, that which rests on the nature of man created by God and that presupposes this nature, i.e., the absolute justice of the created order.

In the second place, there is that which is relatively just, namely, that which, in consideration of reality that no longer conforms to its creator, is just. Brunner points, by way of illustration, to the answer that Jesus gave to the Pharisee's question about Moses' toleration of divorce. Brunner calls this a "concession." This is a relative justice, not as an unavoidable given but as something that is necessary because all of the virtuousness of positive law rests on the restraining influence (*mässigende Anpassung*) of relative justice.[67]

We discover the relativizing of which we are speaking here first of all in Brunner's book *Justice and the Social Order*. We are confronted, however, with an even more radical relativization in Brunner's earlier book *The Divine Imperative*.

Here Brunner emphatically states that God's will cannot be grasped by us in a general principle. We cannot dispose over this will. God is altogether free in relation to us. And the Christian is a free sovereign because he stands *immediately* under the personal command of God in his sovereign freedom. Neither can love hold as such a general principle; instead, God is the one who first defines what love is *in his acts*. True obedience is not in terms of general principles, but of the free, sovereign will of God. A commandment of God can be grasped only in the concrete situation of its being heard. Indeed, in the sense of a general order, the law has the task of preparing for free decision and hearing the concrete divine commandment. It is for

---

[67] Brunner, *Justice and the Social Order*, pp. 110ff.

this reason that the first commandment of Christian ethics is to come to terms with the existing order! Nevertheless, this does not relieve anyone of the duty to ask in the first place for the concrete commandment of God. No one can deduce from a general law in a *logical, casuistic* fashion what he is required to do at a particular moment. Indeed, a situation might present itself in which one had to act contrary to general law. Put otherwise, knowledge of the (completely concrete) commandment of love in a concrete case within sinful reality can break through what is required by a general law. And then for Brunner the creation ordinances as well as the express biblical commandments fall under this judgment. So, for instance, divorce may become a necessity. For a legalistic, casuistic ethics (*gesetzlich-kasuistische Ethik*) this possibility, according to Brunner, does not exist. For it the matter is already settled, that divorce is forbidden under all circumstances, *because it has no court of appeal above the law.* It does not understand that knowledge of the commandment of love — *and that means knowledge of grace* — may in a concrete case transgress a general rule.[68] This conception of the commandment of love easily joins forces with the previously discussed conception of the "commandment of the hour" (*Gebot der Stunde*), according to which God's will comes to us out of historical reality.

From the foregoing it is clear that Brunner, in the last analysis, allows himself to be guided by the dialectical religious ground motive of nature and grace. He distinguishes, namely, between the so-called natural creation ordinances and the Word revelation in its creaturely and thereby continuing form, on the one hand, and the concrete commandment of love as a gift of grace, on the other hand, indeed, in the sense that situations can present themselves in which these two can come to stand in sharp conflict with each other. For Brunner, therefore, there is no *inner* relation between the creation ordinances, on the one side, and the commandment of love, on the other. Thus the former are divorced from the dynamic of the latter. That explains Brunner's assertion that the creation ordinances are intrinsically static. That means, in fact, that in Brunner's thought there is ascribed to natural law a certain independence: knowl-

---

[68] Brunner, *The Divine Imperative,* pp. 83, 90f., 117f., 138f., 354f.

edge of the creation ordinances, as we saw, can function as a *preamble* to understanding the veritable commandment of love. This view of the commandment of love in relation to the creation ordinances cannot truly be understood, furthermore, apart from Brunner's actualistic belief concerning revelation. Brunner, namely, cannot *believe* that God has given us *abiding* ordinances or norms, which he also maintains in his faithfulness. Brunner cannot believe that God reveals himself to us clearly and on a continuing basis, and that this revelation can be known, be it in faith. For him, indeed, the Holy Scriptures are not the true Word of God. Men cannot dispose over the Word. It is and remains God's grace, when our word becomes an instrument of the Word. Even publicly reading the Bible does not mean per se that the Word is being proclaimed. For that matter, the Bible itself is not, simply speaking, the Word of God; it is a human testimony, be it a primal one, to the Word. In us and through us, therefore, it must become a witness. The biblical commandments, therefore, are an indirect revelation and belong as such, as we have seen, to the domain which Brunner has characterized as "law" (*lex*). They too, as such, may be broken by the (concrete) commandment of God.[69]

At bottom we are confronted here with a dualistic belief in God, namely, a faith in God as Creator and a belief in that God who in His grace comes to us in the concrete commandment of love. In addition, both of these, as we saw, can even come to stand in conflict with each other, in which case God as Creator must make way for God as love. The influence of Gnosticism here is difficult to deny.

4. Critical Recapitulation

In the preceding sections we have given attention to a view of the order of justice that has more the character of natural law and one that is more actualistic.

In so far as the thinkers began with super-arbitrary ideas or creaturely constants, they always ascribed to them an unchangeableness, a static character. This showed itself to be the case for Plato because he viewed the world of ideas as a super-

---

[69] *Ibid.*, pp. 135, 143, 524f.

temporal, self-sufficient reality that rested in itself. In Aristotle this was connected with his view that the ideas as formative principles have their deepest ground, their true cause, in absolute, divine reason, which is itself the first, unmoved and as such unchangeable mover of the universe.

These thinkers thereby were confronted inescapably with the problem of relating these more or less rigid ideas to the dynamic of historical reality. Aristotle attempted to build a bridge here by asserting that the ideas, which as such have their origin in absolute reason, are active as formative principles *in* individual things. That could not hinder Aristotle's conception of society from retaining a more or less static character, in that it was altogether oriented to the Greek city state of the time. In Aristotle's thought there is a direct causal relation, we might also say, a continuous line, between absolute reason and the ideas as they are at work in reality. The ideas participate, therefore, directly in absolute reason, but also participate nevertheless in the character of reality.

Considered in this light, the natural law conception of the Stoics can be said to be more "progressive," in so far as it looks beyond the narrow confines of the Greek city state and has a place for the idea of world citizenship, for the rights that accrue to man as such. Nevertheless, in the conception of the Stoics there also appeared a sharp tension between the idea of world citizenship and the institution of the state. This appeared to be particularly the case in the formulation that Seneca gave to Stoic thought. Furthermore, in the Stoic conception of human existence no account could be given in any way of the great variety of structures with which we are confronted in human society. For Seneca also the individual and the state are the two poles between which human life moves, in addition to which the idea of world citizenship in its full sense continued to glimmer as a remote ideal. The tension between the absolute law of nature in its total unchangeableness and the actual course of human society now comes to expression sharply in Christian thinkers such as Augustine and Thomas Aquinas, as a consequence that they situate the unchangeable ideas in God himself. Thomas, tying in with the thought of Aristotle, attempted to resolve this tension by adopting individual principles which, on the one hand, have their ground in God as the creative logos, but which, on the other hand, are unbreakably connected with individual things and operate therein as powers that propel individual things towards their perfection. Nevertheless, Thomas' own conception of justice and society retains a static character, insofar as he orients himself almost exclusively to the hierarchically organized structure of society as it existed in his time, i.e., the unified culture of the Middle Ages as it took shape under the leading of the church. That Thomas went this way can be accounted for most likely in terms of the same factors that were at work in Aristotle. Just as in Aristotle's thought the ideas have their cause in the creative logos as the first, itself unmoved mover of the universe, in Thomas the formative principles of individual things have their origin in God as the creative logos. As such they participate, be it in an analogical fashion, in creative reason; but by the same token they also participate in the rational structure of the logos. In Thomas, therefore, as a result of the unsettling of his Christian idea of creation under the influence of the Aristotelian conception of the logos, there is a danger that the boundaries between the Creator and the creation will be obscured, with a resulting ascription of a certain independency to reality, considered to be natural, rational, and also rationally penetrable, with reference to the Word revelation and as a consequence also with reference to the central commandment of love. This danger also includes, of course, the natural existence of man, which is also considered to be essentially rational and rationally penetrable.

In order to avoid the element of "rigidification" that is apparently involved in the traditional conception of natural law, Brunner appealed to the commandment of love, thereby making a leap from a more rationalistic or intellectualistic to a more voluntaristic view concerning God's will for the world. As a consequence, however, there appeared to arise insoluble tensions between the creation ordinances and the concrete commandment of love, tensions which seemed to have their source and explanation in a dualistic belief in God.

Barth and Ellul attempted to discover a solution for this problem by placing right and justice on an exclusively Christological foundation, that is to say, to see both in the light of the judgment on this world that comes in Christ. For an idea of an order of creation that is upheld in Christ, in which justice too would have its foundation, there remained little or no place in these thinkers. In the case of Ellul this resulted in what is, in point of fact, a nearly pragmatic view of actually binding positive law: man judges according to a criterion of justice that he formulates according to how he senses the situation and with the insight he possesses into the currently dominant relationships. From a biblical standpoint this solution is unsatisfactory, for in it there is scarcely any account given of the biblical teaching that God, in all circumstances, directly, in particular in his Word, is present in this world and that we are required to act everywhere *coram deo*.

Finally, *Western humanistic thought,* in so far as it has been willing to hear of a natural law, has sought to discover its ground in (creative) human reason. Even there it has been impossible to arrive at an internally consistent view of justice and of (positive) law. Even less has it been possible there to render an account of the great variety of structures in human society. Western humanistic thought oscillates in a continuing dialectic movement between the two poles of the individual and the community (state), without being able to bring them to a real inner reconciliation.

5. Justice in a Pluralistic Society

As a consequence, the question bears in upon us, whether it is possible to arrive at an intrinsically more cohesive, homogenous conception of justice and right, in which the previously established tensions are resolved, at least in principle. In conclusion, I shall make an attempt to sketch such a view.

*

In the line of Augustine, in the first place, and that of many Christian thinkers after him, I shall take my point of departure in the confession of the absolute sovereignty of God, as Creator, as that is again revealed to us in its fullness in Christ Jesus. This confession carries with it the acknowledgment of the complete lack of self-sufficiency of reality, in which we ourselves dwell and of which we ourselves are a part. Everything in this reality points outside and above itself, as such comprising a single great coherent whole. Furthermore, that coherent whole, in its totality, is not self-sufficient; it points beyond itself to an origin from which it derives its meaning, to God as the Creator of the universe in its inexhaustible variety of organic and inorganic things, plants and animals, human life, planets, the world of angels, etc. Nothing exists in itself.[70]

*

The foregoing implies that reality, in which we move, is not a chaos, as Brunner has so aptly observed, but an ordered cosmos. All subjective happening in the world occurs on the foundation of, or within the framework of, an intrinsically connected order, which has its origin in God's word of creation. Everywhere we are confronted with ordinances of a super-arbitrary nature. Without them reality would be incomprehensible; it would collapse into formlessness (an *apeiron*), into nothingness. Abraham Kuyper speaks of these ordinances "as the constant will of the Omnipresent and Almighty God, who at every instant is determining the course of life, ordaining its laws and continually binding us by His divine authority."[71] We can also put it this way, that the ordinances referred to are the instruments with which God governs the world.

*

We saw earlier that Augustine and Thomas Aquinas situate their creation ideas in God himself: they comprise part of God's essence. If I have understood Gilson correctly, he claims that Duns Scotus takes a point of view on this question which in some respects differs from that of Augustine and Thomas. Duns

[70] *The Holy Bible.* Furthermore, Augustine, *Confessions,* particularly book XII; Abraham Kuyper, *Souvereiniteit in eigen kring: Rede ter inwijding van de Vrije Universiteit* (2nd ed.; Amsterdam, 1880), pp. 9, 30, 32, 33, 35, 37; Kuyper, *Dictaten Dogmatiek,* VIII: *Locus de Magistratu* (unpublished, 1893; also Grand Rapids [Mich.]: J. B. Hulst, 1910), p. 148; Kuyper, *De Gemeene Gratie* (3 vols.; 3rd. ed.; Kampen: J. H. Kok, 1932), II, 48, 86; III, 13–14, 134, 167; Kuyper, *Calvinism: Six Stone Foundation Lectures* (Grand Rapids: Eerdmans, 1931; 1943), 45f., 53, 112f.; Kuyper, *Antirevolutionaire Staatkunde* (2 vols.; Kampen: J. H. Kok, 1916–1917), I, 11, 33, 261; H. Dooyeweerd, *A New Critique,* I, 101.
[71] Kuyper, *Calvinism,* pp. 70–71.

Scotus seems to be inclined to view the ideas themselves as creations, thus as entities that are located between God and his creatures. Gilson describes the ideas as they are conceived by Duns Scotus as ". . . the *creatures* themselves as *creatable* by God, and existing in Him in virtue of their concepts as possibles. In this doctrine, as in St. Bonaventure and St. Thomas, the idea has its source in the depths of the divine essence, but now *it bears no longer on this essence, were it only as capable of participation, it bears directly on the eventual participations.* It is by His essence, certainly, that God knows possible creatures, *but His ideas of these creatures are not views of His essence nor even of its imitability, but of the imitations.* Thus in Scotism *the essence of God, taken in itself, is wholly enclosed in its own splendour,* unclouded by the shadows which the multiplicity of its finite imitations might cast upon it, even were these considered as simply realizables; *God conceives the ideas because he thinks of creatures, although it is only with respect to Himself that He thinks of them.*"[72] (Italics mine) In a footnote, Gilson adds, "Thus in Duns Scotus there is an eternal *generation* of the intelligible being *of things which will one day be created, prior to their creation itself. The divine production of the idea is a kind of eternal prelude to temporal creation.*"[73] (Italics mine)

On the one hand, Duns Scotus no longer gives the ideas a place in the divine essence; on the other hand, he apparently hesitates to give them a place simply among created things. It

[72] Gilson, *The Spirit of Medieval Philosophy*, p. 160. Original French: ". . . les créatures elles-mêmes en tant que créables par Dieu et existant en lui par leurs concepts à titre de possibles. Dans cette doctrine, bien qu'elle ait sa source aux profondeurs de l'essence divine comme chez Bonaventure et saint Thomas, l'idée ne porte donc plus sur cette essence, ne fût-ce qu'en tant que participable, mais directement sur ses participations éventuelles. C'est bien par son essence que Dieu connait les créatures possibles, mais les idées qu'il a de ces créatures ne sont pas des vues de son essence, ni même de son imitabilité, mais bien de ses imitations. Ainsi, dans le scotisme, l'essence de Dieu prise en soi se renferme dans sa splendeur; elle est pure de l'ombre portée que pourrait projeter sur elle la multiplicité de ses imitations finies, mêmes considérées comme simplement réalisables; Dieu conçoit les idées parce qu'il pense les créatures, bien qu'il ne les pense que par rapport à soi." Gilson, *L'esprit de la philosophie médiévale* (2nd rev. ed.; Paris: J. Vrin, 1944, 1969), pp. 167–168.

[73] Gilson, *The Spirit of Medieval Philosophy*, p. 460.

seems to us to be necessary here to make a choice, in view of the fact that a clear distinction must be made between the Creator and his creation. That forces us to the conclusion that the law or the order for reality in its factual, subjective existence has its place within what is created. In analogy to what Thomas asserts concerning the unbreakable correlation between individual things and the formative principles that are at work in them, I believe that reality in its factual, subjective existence and the creation ordinances holding for it are given to us in an unbreakable correlation, that is to say, that there are no subjective, factual phenomena without an order that holds for them and that there are no true ordinances apart from a factual reality to which they pertain. With an eye to this state of affairs we may speak of *con-creation.* That is to say, in the same breath, that the creation ordinances or creation-ideas are completely characterized by the lack of self-sufficiency and are completely taken up in the fundamental dynamism of all creation. They take their place of honor *in* the history that the creation undergoes. The creation ordinances are powers established and continually maintained by God in creation, by means of which he gives natural as well as normative guidance to the world, and energizes, determines, gives direction, upholds, and preserves it in its activity. "Thou didst establish the earth, and it stands. They stand this day according to Thine ordinances, for all things are Thy servants" (Psalm 119:90b-91; NAS Version).

*

This order, this law of God for the creation, is perfect. That is to say, it does not manifest any lacunas and is applicable to all situations, even those in the world as it has been broken by sin. That already appears in the warning of judgment incorporated in the commandment given in Paradise (Genesis 2:17). God pursues man with his original law of creation to the farthest reaches of his existence. That Adam and Eve experienced right away, even as Cain did in a subsequent phase. According to the express witness of Genesis 1:31, God perfectly equipped his creation. He did not "miscalculate" in any way. There is no place, therefore, for any transgression of the original order of creation as the result of the entrance of sin in the world, in the sense that Brunner considers it necessary. That is not even the

CARL A. RUDISILL LIBRARY
LENOIR RHYNE COLLEGE

case with regard to Moses' toleration of divorce, which Brunner uses as an illustration. The Swiss social ethicist Rudolf Grob has correctly pointed out that the commandment concerning the sanctity of marriage has retained its force even in the world as it has been distorted by sin. If the Mosaic law held out to a woman the possibility of divorcing her husband, it did this, as Grob says, in recognition of the fact that such a marriage had already been dissolved by unfaithfulness. Such a provision of the law has the function of protecting the woman. This ordinance of the civil magistrate had the effect of alleviating the consequences of sin; but it did not at all imply a condoning of sin. The intrinsic validity of the original law of God is not at all weakened by such a protective measure. One who obtains a divorce from his wife, even if he has fulfilled all his civil obligations before the law and has the permission of a human court, is not exonerated thereby before the judgment seat of God. In the eyes of God he remains, says Grob, both in life and in death bound to this woman.[74] For any concession in the sense intended by Brunner there is here no place.

*

The foregoing implies, at the same time, that it makes no sense to make a distinction between the enduring, supposedly static creation ordinances as an expression of God's creative sovereignty and the concrete commandment of love as an expression of God's grace. In the Holy Scriptures the law of God is revealed to us, instead, as itself a gift of God's grace, which is not intended to place a constricting circle around life but to allow us to break out into open places and to make us wise.[75] It is the case that the ordinances of creation find their realization in the central commandment of love, while these same creation ordinances, in turn, may be seen as typical expressions, typical manifestations, of this central commandment. Together they comprise the single, indivisible, original order of creation. In the creation order, upheld in Christ, the fullness of God's love expresses itself, just as we can say that in this order, upheld in Christ, it is the case that the fullness of God's justice comes

---

[74] Rudolf Grob, *Aufbau der Gemeinschaft: Grundzüge einer reformierten Sozialethik* (Zürich: Zwingli Verlag, 1940), p. 32.
[75] Psalm 119: 29, 32, 37, 45, 98, 100.

to expression. In their fullness, God's love and his justice coincide completely with each other. That becomes clear in the suffering and death of Jesus Christ on the cross. Redemption, as a re-creation, also stands, therefore, in relation to the fullness of every created thing.[76] In this connection one may not speak of a higher and a lower realm. In all of reality the complete love as well as the complete justice of God hold in a dynamic fashion, and, in addition, there is a universal expression of the conflict between the Kingdom of God and the kingdom of darkness.[77] Both the central commandment of love and the creation ordinances founded therein are characterized, therefore, both by constancy and dynamism. It is thus very meaningful to speak in this connection of a constant dynamism in the order of creation.

*

The order of creation is, therefore, the law-conformable framework within which a subjective event in the world — be it one of "dead" matter, of the world of plants and animals, or of human existence — occurs and reveals itself. The order of creation involves the mandate to preserve and to build in the world. As this mandate is fulfilled, the creation order itself comes to a dynamic development. As such the order of creation is, at the same time, the horizon of human experience, against which the individual phenomena stand out in their variety of structures. Without this structural horizon of experience reality, as earlier remarked, would be indefiniteness (an *apeiron*), something indeterminate and meaningless and therefore also unknowable.

*

Now in this connection it is necessary to distinguish further between the creation ordinances for nature, i.e., for the world of natural inorganic things, of plants and animals, as well as the natural aspects of human existence, and the creation ordinances for human life. While the former are given us in a direct observation of the subjective phenomena, the latter are given us in the form of principles, ones furthermore that are operating concretely. That means that the creation ordinances for human so-

---

[76] Cf., e.g., Eph. 1:10; Col. 1:20; Heb. 2:8; 1 John 2:2.
[77] Cf., e.g., Heb. 4:12.

ciety are dependent, among other things, upon human forming for their concrete validity. We may also put the matter this way: Man is called as the co-laborer with God to give concrete form to creation also as to its law- or norm-side, as to its orderly side. As such he too bears responsibility for the concrete structures. In this sense he has dominion over these structures. This has its deeper ground in the circumstance that in the depth of his existence man, in his ego, transcends all particular structures, as well as these structures in their mutual relationships.

The latter does not imply, of course, that man becomes the true standard for judging the truth or the usefulness of the social structures, in the spirit of Western humanism. Even in the transcendence referred to above man remains bound, to be specific, to the cosmic order, which embraces his entire existence and which has its unitary ground, as we saw, in the all-embracing commandment of love to God and to one's neighbor, in the mandate to build and to preserve the creation. The social structures remain thus the normative framework within which man continually, in a typically qualified fashion, can answer to the said creation mandate and can serve his neighbor.

*

Man is called therefore to give concrete form to the so-called structure-norms or structure-principles, which hold, by virtue of the order of creation, for the various societal relationships: the family and marriage, the state, the school association, a music group, a business, etc. Nowhere is he simply left to his own devices.

In this concrete forming of such structural norms man is invested with *authority,* which at bottom he does not derive, as Western humanism teaches, from himself or from those who have called him to his place of authority (the people, or whatever) but from God. Authority indeed has its deepest ground in the divine world order. It has as such an official and therein also an independent character. That remains also the case, if in its concrete organs it comes into being with the co-operation of those who are subject to it. Further, this authority retains its validity independently of whether it is carried out for better or for worse.[78] The true task of those in authority is one of estab-

[78] Cf. 1 Pet. 2:18.

lishing norms for various communities, in an ethical, juridical, economic, social, aesthetic fashion, etc. This task must be carried out in subjection to the normative structural principles that hold for those communities and with the recognition of the required margins of freedom that must serve to allow the responsibility of the individual members of the community, as co-laborers in the creation, to come to its rights.

This authority makes itself felt in many ways in many kinds of communities. It continually manifests therein too a unique structure, which corresponds with the unique character of the various communities. This holds for authority in the family, the school, the business undertaking, the orchestra, the state, the university, etc. In these communities we have to do with varying structures of authority which, by reason of their typical unique natures cannot be reduced to each other, not even with respect to their forms. For each of these authority structures requirements are set. To each applies a peculiar kind of normativity. As such they cannot be subordinated to, but only co-ordinated with, each other.

The latter can be understood only in the light of the Gospel, which teaches that it is only Christ as the Word become flesh to whom universal authority has been given.[78] This involves that by nature, i.e., by virtue of the divine order, every earthly authority is a limited one.[79]

By means of this it becomes understandable that in humanistic circles, as the result of the rejection of a concentration point for reality that stands outside of reality and as a result of the fact that there is a law of concentration inescapably at work in the cosmos, even in society, the attempt has been made again and again to seek such a concentration point within society itself. As a result an exclusive emphasis is placed, either on the individual or on the (state) community, as we observed in Hugo Grotius, John Locke, and Jean Jacques Rousseau. This is even the case with thinkers who appear to have their eyes open for the state of affairs I have described, such as the French philosopher and sociologist of law Georges Gurvitch (1894–1968) and the British political thinker Harold Laski (1893–1950).[80]

*

[79] Cf., e.g., Matt. 28:18; Phil. 2:10; Col. 1:15ff.
[80] Kuyper, *Souvereiniteit in eigen kring*, p. 11. For an exposition of

The preceding, of course, also has its consequences for our view concerning justice and positive law.

Beforehand we spoke of the fullness of justice, which is given to us in the creation order preserved for us in Christ. This justice in its fullness appeared to coincide with love in its fullness. Similarly we may speak of the fullness of beauty given us in creation. Friedrich Schelling was justified to a certain degree in saying that world history is a work of art. He simply made the mistake of absolutizing this beauty at the expense, e.g., of justice and love. Even at that it is meaningful to speak of the extent and the power of the Kingdom of God, which embraces the entire creation, and of the economy of this same kingdom. The great Lutheran philosopher of law and of the state Friedrich Julius Stahl even spoke of ideas of an economy of the world (*weltökonomische Ideen*).[81]

In this reality we have to do, however, not only with a fullness, with a totality, but also with a diversity. In this connection, besides the aforementioned things and societal communities which are distinguished as to their nature, mention can also be made of the (modal) aspects or ways in which reality exists, which are also distinguished as to their nature and structure. Things and societal structures function *within* these aspects, e.g., the arithmetical, the spatial, the energetic, the biotic, the psychical, the logical, the lingual, the economic, the aesthetic, and the ethical aspects.

In this series of (modal) ways of existing or aspects the juridical aspect of reality also has its own place.

One of the characteristics of these (modal) aspects is that there can be distinguished within them a so-called subjective, factual side and a law side. This I have already done with reference to cosmic or created reality in general. In addition, we

the views of Gurvitch, see J. D. Dengerink, "De structuur van het recht en de taak der rechtssociologie: Een critische analyse van de denkbeelden van Georges Gurvitch," *Philosophia Reformata*, XXV (1960), 46–77; and for a profound analysis of Laski's thoughts see the dissertation of Bernard Zijlstra, *From Pluralism to Collectivism: The Development of Harold Laski's Political Thought* (Assen: Van Gorcum, 1968).

[81] Cf., e.g., Friedrich Julius Stahl, *Rechts- und Staatslehre auf der Grundlage christlicher Weltanschauung* (3rd ed.; Heidelberg, 1854–1856), I, 76–79.

have the peculiar situation we established earlier, that the laws or norms of the so-called spiritual or normative aspects of reality are given to us only in principle and as such require positivizing by those who are authorized to do so.

What we have said holds as well for the juridical aspects of reality. Within this aspect also we have to do with the distinction between a law-side and a subject-side, and on the law-side furthermore with the distinction between the legal principles and the actual form in which these principles have their positive validity.

From what I have previously remarked it may be concluded that the legal principles in question may not be conceived as ethical postulates nor even less as a complex of (juridical) values that in one fashion or another have to be brought into contact with concrete legal reality. Instead, they are dynamic forces, which assume validity concretely in the entire process of the formation of law, even though the ones who are involved in making laws are not always aware of the fact.[82]

In this connection it must be expressly stated, furthermore, that within the juridical aspect of reality we have to do with a great diversity of legal orders, e.g., law proper to the state, civil law, law proper to associations, ecclesiastical law, corporation law, law proper to schools, laws proper to universities, and all kinds of contracts (contracts of sale, rental contracts, etc.). For each of these legal orders there holds too a unique complex of legal principles, which are adapted in a typical fashion to the unique character of the arrangements proper to them. It is impossible to approach all of the legal patterns we have mentioned in the same way, even though they together function in the same aspect. Nor is it possible to lump them together under a single heading, without doing injustice to their ever unique qualifications. That is to say too, that no single unit of society can lay claim to having a monopoly in establishing justice in the world — not even the state. Just as

---

[82] As is well known, the existence of super-arbitrary principles of law is sharply denied by the positivistic school of jurisprudence, whose history goes back to the beginning of the 19th century. For the positivists every provision of the law derives its validity from the form of the law itself in which it has come into existence, that is to say, from a competent law making body.

soon as the government of a state believes, though it be with the best intentions, that it is called to determine and to establish the pattern of law for the entire society it moves, *nolens volens* in a totalitarian direction. By reason of the order of creation, there are a great number of responsibilities that are distinct in nature and that are therefore intrinsically limited in scope.

Among other things, it is a task for the science of law to track down the legal principles in question and to formulate them more sharply. It should also ascertain whether these principles have sufficiently penetrated the fabric of the order of law as it actually pertains. In this the science of jurisprudence, along with others, has at the same time a critical task to fulfill.

In the lawmaking process too the law of inertia appears to be at work again and again, with all of the injustice that flows from it. We then have to cope with the phenomenon of rigidification. This rigidifying is, to be sure, not, as Brunner thinks, a result of the inelasticity of so-called natural law or that of enduring principles of law; instead, it is a consequence of the slothfulness of the human spirit which, consciously or unconsciously, divorces itself from the dynamic inherent in the legal principles, a dynamic that requires that the order of law as it actually pertains must constantly be adjusted to new situations and developments that appear or, even further, that can be expected. With reference to the lawmaking process too it is the case that "to govern is to foresee" (*gouverner est prévoir*). In addition, we should not fix our attention solely on relationships within nations but also upon those between nations, because we are faced with the demand for justice not only in national but also international relations. It is of the utmost importance that on the international level thinking in terms of a struggle for power be replaced with thinking in terms of international justice. If this is to be accomplished, however, there is a pressing need for reflection on the unique character and the intrinsic limits of this international law, which appears in essence to have a political nature, if new totalitarian pretensions, on an international scale, are to be avoided. In addition, it is also a "must" to reflect on justice in its inexhaustible structural diversity. To this end Christians, of all people, because of their insight into the structures of the cosmos and in terms of their unique view of history, can and must make an essential, even an indispensable, contribution. They may, to be exact, not forget that they have here to do with God's world, which because of the rebellion of man was indeed threatened with destruction, but which, because of the work of Christ in his suffering and death, is moving towards a new destiny by way of the last judgment, and *remains* therefore God's world.

Index of Persons